# BROKEN

## MY CAMPAIGN FOR CHILD ADVOCACY, PARENTAL EQUALITY AND FAMILY BALANCE

JOSEPH P. COWLES

LUMINARE PRESS
WWW.LUMINAREPRESS.COM

Broken: My campaign for Child Advocacy, Parental Equality and
Family Balance
© 2017 Joseph P. Cowles

All rights reserved. This book or any portion thereof may not be reproduced or used in any manner whatsoever without the express written permission of the publisher, except for the use of brief quotations in a book review.

Printed in the United States of America

Cover design: Claire Last
Cover photo: Joseph P. Cowles
Cover photo editing: Catherine M. Eskew

Luminare Press
438 Charnelton St., Suite 101
Eugene, OR 97401
www.luminarepress.com

LCCN: 2017932955
ISBN: 978-1-944733-17-9

*My mother, who raised me with love,
and my son, the greatest gift in my life!*

## CONTENTS

- Introduction . . . . . . . . . . . . . . . . . . . . . . . 1
- Everyone's Loss . . . . . . . . . . . . . . . . . . . . . 5
- The Writing on the Wall . . . . . . . . . . . . . . . 9
- Crossing Paths . . . . . . . . . . . . . . . . . . . . . 17
- The Gift . . . . . . . . . . . . . . . . . . . . . . . . . 22
- Competitive Parenting . . . . . . . . . . . . . . . 28
- The Split . . . . . . . . . . . . . . . . . . . . . . . . 33
- A Squandered Solution . . . . . . . . . . . . . . . 39
- The Settlement . . . . . . . . . . . . . . . . . . . . 43
- The Web . . . . . . . . . . . . . . . . . . . . . . . . 47
- The Hired Gun . . . . . . . . . . . . . . . . . . . . 55
- Bouncing Back . . . . . . . . . . . . . . . . . . . . 63
- Finding Time . . . . . . . . . . . . . . . . . . . . . 67
- The Bitter Truth . . . . . . . . . . . . . . . . . . . 71
- The Last Resort . . . . . . . . . . . . . . . . . . . 78
- The Gap . . . . . . . . . . . . . . . . . . . . . . . . 91
- The Squeaky Wheel . . . . . . . . . . . . . . . . . 99
- The Workgroup . . . . . . . . . . . . . . . . . . . 109
- The Turn . . . . . . . . . . . . . . . . . . . . . . . 119
- A Voice . . . . . . . . . . . . . . . . . . . . . . . . 133
- A Better Way . . . . . . . . . . . . . . . . . . . . 143

# Introduction

This book is about child advocacy, parental equality, and family balance.

I am a single father with a ten-year-old son. Due to life's circumstances, I was raised without a father and without the support, guidance, and love a father can provide. For this reason, I am determined to play an active role in my son's life and to give him what I did not have.

Although I am six feet three inches tall and weigh 230 pounds, I have been pushed, hit, stabbed, stalked, and held against my will by my son's mother, who is half my weight. The only defense I had was to exit the relationship. My mission has been to weather the storm through the transition to single parenthood and to preserve my connection to my son. However, there has been a monumental barrier to my progress that has discriminated against me as a parent, even though I am a good father.

Oregon Revised Statute (ORS) 107.169(3) states, "The court shall not order joint custody, unless both parents agree to the terms and conditions of the order." The rationale of the court is that if parents cannot agree to work together, the court must award all major decision-making authority to one parent. The theory is that, for the sake of the child, this process will minimize conflict between the parents. The court's decision is typically permanent from the onset of custody to the advent of the child's adulthood.

The reason for most custody disputes is because a parent may feel scorned or vengeful due to a separation. Sole custody is a potent vehicle for revenge and usually not because a parent is unfit to make rational decisions. A child usually feels the tension between parents in a custody dispute and may feel that they are the cause of it. The long-term effects can be damaging to a child. He or she can lose the family balance of having both parents' involvement, and it can seem like one parent owns them, while the other parent is pushed out.

It is common to hear about deadbeat parents, but we don't often hear about parental alienation. Sole custody is a familiar cause of parental alienation. It can supply the sole custodial parent the power to shut out the other parent. This is also a reason many distressed parents demand sole custody.

Sole custody does currently have a purpose. It is for extreme cases where one parent is abusive, neglectful, psychiatrically unstable, addicted to drugs, or not around. Sole custody should not be determined simply because one parent demands the entitlement.

Instead of assisting parents through a difficult transition, the current law has the effect of pouring gasoline onto a fire. It pits the parents against each other in a winner-takes-all cage fight with the child as the trophy. This is referred to as a zero-sum game. One parent gains all the custodial responsibilities, and the other parent loses all the custodial responsibilities.

In this book, I will share my story, address problems in current state family law, and offer rational solutions that will better assist families through this difficult life transition.

CHAPTER ONE

# Everyone's Loss

When I was a young boy, I yearned for my father's attention. We were a military family of eleven children (seven girls and four boys), and I was the youngest. My father was a civil engineer and colonel in the US Army. He traveled frequently, including multiple tours of duty in Vietnam, where he witnessed the horror of war. My mother told me he was never the same after Vietnam. I was born in the summer of 1970, shortly after his last tour of duty there.

When I was six years old, my father separated from my mother after nineteen years of marriage. At the time, we were living in Oahu, Hawaii, on a US Army base. He offered to relocate us to wherever my mother felt most comfortable starting over. She was not interested in moving back to North Dakota, where she grew up. She felt like a failure in comparison to her four sisters. They all still lived in the same area, they were all still married, and they had thirty children between them.

My mother remembered driving through a place called Eugene, Oregon, when she was in college. She appreciated the vibrant shades of green in the valley, the mountains that lie to the east and west, and the ocean nearby. Without knowing a soul there, my mother took a leap of faith and relocated to Eugene with ten children. My eldest brother had just moved away to start college at the University of Washington. It was the summer of 1976.

Some of us children were very excited for the move. Especially my middle brother, who was a blond-haired haole boy (non-native Hawaiian). He was picked on daily at school by the native Hawaiian children. My mother enticed me for the move by mentioning there were cherry trees in the yard of our new home. But when we arrived, I was underwhelmed by the taste of pie cherries.

After the separation and divorce, my absentee father would visit us once a year for about a week. We all longed for that time to come. My loyal mother would draw a diagonal line through the calendar date each morning she awoke and another before she slept to mark an X. This was her way of feeling one day closer to seeing my father again. Instead of dating, she chose to pray and maintain her faith that my father would come to his senses and return home for good.

During my father's short visits, he would play the guitar and sing while we would all listen. He could play almost anything that involved strings or keys. As he captured our attention by playing music, we would try to capture his attention in our own ways. My closest sibling in age was my brother, who was much smarter than I. He showed an interest in playing the guitar, and, for that reason, he gained my father's undivided attention through lessons. I tried to compete in different ways but exasperated my father more than anything. I could never seem to find my niche with him.

During my adolescence, my father moved from Hawaii to Pennsylvania, to Illinois, and then to Germany on military assignments. In Germany, he remarried to a woman we had never met. After a couple of years, he divorced again. After that, my father retired from the military and accepted a position with a multinational civil engineering firm and was based in Somalia. At the age of thirteen, I got the news that my father was in poor health. He flew back to Germany from Somalia to have a CAT scan. The scan revealed a malignant brain tumor, believed to have been caused by Agent Orange. His time on earth was limited.

When given the news, my mother had my eldest sister fly to Germany to retrieve my father. After his arrival home, he deteriorated each day. It was difficult to watch such a strong man have the life sucked out of him. I remember him trying to speak his thoughts and struggling to find his words. I could only imagine his frustration and fear.

In a short time, my father was unable to speak or walk. The atrophy was substantial. I recall having a private moment to speak with him while he lay unconscious in the hospice bed in my mother's bedroom. I told him that I loved him, that I missed him, and that I could not understand how he could bring eleven children into the world with my mother and then leave them. I value that moment when I expressed my feelings, but I will never know if he heard me. Nonetheless, it was good for me. A few days later, my father passed away.

When my father passed away, I was outside the house and sitting on the curb. It was summertime and twelve days before my fourteenth birthday. My middle brother came out to get me and gave me a lashing for not being present for my father's last breath. I felt the guilt and the loss.

CHAPTER TWO

# The Writing on the Wall

When my family relocated from Oahu to Eugene, the neighborhood we moved to was thriving. We had around three dozen kids on our street, including my clan. In the evenings, we played games like kick the can, run sheep run, detectives, and swinging statues. Danny Ainge (the only athlete in history to be a first-team All-American in football, basketball, and baseball) was going into his senior year at the local high school with my oldest sister. Life was pretty good for us, but my mother suffered from a broken heart.

I would sleep on my mother's floor to keep her company, and she would tell me stories of her childhood on the farm in North Dakota. The farm had no running water and was in a town of about eighty inhabitants. Her stories helped me appreciate what I had. In my upbringing, my mother did the best she could. Raising a large family by herself and keeping a full-time job was almost more than any human could endure. She enrolled in courses at the University of Oregon to obtain the tools to cope with her new reality. She also found serenity at a church up the road from our house.

Through the church, my mother befriended a retired couple. The relationship proved to be very beneficial for me. The old-timer husband took an active role in my upbringing and taught me how to garden, fish, play tennis, swing a golf club, and play penny poker. But, most important of all, he taught me respect. When I was a young lad, he would tease me about the girls. When I hit puberty, he told me to keep that thing in my pants! He gave me more guidance and support than many kids in my neighborhood had.

After our first summer in Eugene, I started first grade. My vivid memory often takes me back to that period. My classroom was in an annex building, and classmates had to share double desks. My desk neighbor ended up being my arch nemesis all the way through primary school. Our feud started on one of the first days of school, when the boy purposefully wiped his booger on my hand-me-down jacket. I punched him in the nose for it.

Hand-me-down clothes were common for me because I was the youngest in my family. It was not uncommon for me to wear my brothers' underwear and to have to fold the waistline over three times to make them fit or to wear my sisters' tennis shoes because their feet were closer to my size. My nemesis classmate loved the days when I came to school looking like an orphan with tattered clothes and colorful clown shoes.

There was a particular girl in my grade that I struggled with as well. This childhood tormenter would eventually become my adulthood tormenter, as well as my wife and the mother of my son. I will refer to her in this book by her childhood nickname, "Noni." Noni also came from a single-mother household and had a sister who was ten months older, whom I got along with much better. Because I had seven sisters, many of my friends growing up were also girls. I felt I could relate better with females than most boys my age. Nevertheless, I could never relate to or connect with Noni growing up.

One incident, which I would rather forget, was in the sixth grade at outdoor school. It was the first time many of us children had spent multiple nights away from our families. I was excited to have that independence. However, my experience ended up much different than I had anticipated. I had a crush on a girl that liked another boy, the forts we built were destroyed by the heavy rains, and I got my ass kicked by the very girl I tried to avoid, Noni.

The setting was in the woods along a creek side. I was with five girls, and we were playing under the canopy of fir trees. Four of the girls were my good friends and the fifth, my worst nightmare. We were all having fun and being goofy when a switch flipped inside Noni, and she demanded that I fight her. She swatted my ball cap off my head, repeatedly pushed me in the chest, and kept slapping me across the face. I was hard-wired to never hit a girl and I did not retaliate. Instead, I absorbed the humiliation and wanted nothing more than to go home. Later, I confronted

Noni and asked her why she treated me so poorly. Her justification was that I had said boys could do things that girls could not do. However, I did not remember it that way.

The last childhood confrontation I had with Noni was during the next school year when we were in seventh grade reading class together. I was sitting at the desk in front of her. When I turned in my chair to speak with another student, she stabbed me in the hand with her number-two pencil. The graphite punctured my skin and broke off in my left index finger. After the wound had healed over, the graphite remnants in it left a permanent tattoo on my finger. From that point forward, I avoided Noni at all costs. She scared the hell out of me. We were also in very different places in our lives. She was a physically maturing young woman who dated older men, and I was still just a boy.

Two years later, I started high school and hit my stride. I grew from five feet nine to six feet three inches tall, threw on fifty pounds of muscle, and excelled as a soccer goalkeeper. My ride was a Volkswagen camper bus, and my girlfriend was my best friend. Life was everything a teenager could hope for.

While I was thriving in my high-school bubble, Noni ran away from home to live with her boyfriend, who was much older. At first, they disappeared to El Salvador, where he was from, but then came back so Noni could complete her diploma.

Because my birthday is in the summertime, I graduated from high school at age seventeen. At the time, my greatest passions were playing soccer and visiting new places. I got to do both, right out of high school, when I was accepted to be a Rotary Foreign Exchange student in Brazil for one year. It was a dream come true and a wonderful experience that I would recommend for any adventurous youngster.

When I returned to Eugene from Brazil, I started courses at the local community college and competed in track and field. From there, I attended several different universities and took a semester off to backpack through Central America. I was on the six-year plan and finally got my bachelor of arts degree in education in 1995. At the time, I thought I wanted to be a teacher in physical education and a soccer coach, but Brazil kept beckoning me to return. For the next three years after college, I followed the sun and had the best of both worlds. Through the spring and summer months, I lived in Oregon and worked outdoors. Through the autumn and winter months, I escaped to Brazil and worked as a fitness trainer.

While I was living the life of a nomad, Noni was living a life of terror. It was the horrendous rape and murder of her older sister that would deeply affect her already tormented soul. She was just twenty-one years old; her sister was only twenty-two when her life was taken from her.

The setting was a warm summer's afternoon in a Portland suburb. At the time of the crime, Noni's sister was engaged to a young man from an upper-class neighborhood and she was visiting his family's home.

A neighbor boy came knocking on the door and asked to speak with her fiancé's younger sister. Nobody was at the house except Noni's sister, so the boy returned home. A short time later, the boy came back and knocked on the door again. Noni's sister opened the door, just as she did the first time. This time, the boy forced his way in. She was on the telephone with her fiancé and the boy abruptly disconnected the phone.

Her fiancé called 9-1-1 after they were disconnected, but it was too late. By the time the police arrived, the deadly predator had brutally raped and murdered Noni's sister beyond description. After the horrendous act of violence, the murderer returned home, took a shower, and spent the rest of the day at the fair with his friends. Steve Mayes of the *Oregonian* newspaper reported the following:

> Victim was staying overnight at a friend's home in Wilsonville. Predator went to the house looking for a teenage girl he knew. Victim answered the door and told him the girl was not there.
>
> Predator decided to rape Victim. He went home and got a Boy Scout knife that had a small, dull blade. After determining Victim was alone, he forced his way into the house. She was on the phone with her fiancé, who overheard the confrontation. Victim screamed, 'What do you want? Please don't hurt me.' The phone went dead. Her fiancé called 9-1-1.

When Predator put down the knife to take his clothes off, Victim grabbed the weapon, cut his hand, thumb and fingers and tried to stab him in the chest.

The rape had not gone as planned. Predator decided to kill Victim to prevent her from reporting the crime. He repeatedly stabbed her throat, cutting so deeply he almost decapitated her.

Afterward, Predator took a shower and spent the rest of the day at the Clackamas County Fair with friends. A tip led police to Predator, who eventually confessed.

In my opinion, if someone purposefully takes the life of an innocent human being, they should forfeit their own. In many countries, one would be instantly executed for such a crime. However, in this great country, our laws are made by attorneys for the benefit of attorneys, and any outcome is possible. In this case, the predator was tried as a minor and given a sentence of fifty years in state prison. His family has been appealing the ruling ever since.

I imagine it has been very difficult for the murdered girl's family to move on and find closure. They must repeatedly relive the horror through the appellate courts, while their tax dollars are housing, educating, and putting food in the mouth of the animal that took their loved one's life.

After the tragedy, I did not have the opportunity to

express my sympathy to the victim's family. It would be selfish for me to believe that my sympathies would have any meaning or significance to the family anyway. Those who knew the victim felt the shock and sorrow, as did the rest of our community. The victim was a beautiful young woman who had the rest of her life ahead of her.

CHAPTER THREE
# Crossing Paths

It was not until I was thirty-four years old that I would see Noni again. She had moved to Costa Rica following her sister's murder and then to Colorado, where she resided for many years. After another dysfunctional relationship, she relocated back to Eugene. At the time, I worked in Eugene in outside sales for a Fortune 100 company while I was completing my executive MBA program.

We ran into each other at a neighborhood pizza parlor and exchanged telephone numbers. The exchange felt odd to me since I had never connected with her, but I felt like we had some catching up to do. Later, we arranged a walk with our dogs and met on the bike path along the riverside. There was very little communication as we walked, and she compulsively focused on commanding her wolf-mix dog. The experience was incredibly awkward, and it was the last I saw her for another year.

The following summer, one of my best friends was living in the makeshift apartment that I had in the upstairs of my house. He repeatedly invited me to attend a yoga class with him at a local studio. He said that Noni was also a student there and that she kept asking about me. My consistent reply was that I was not interested. However, after many invites, I decided to attend class one evening. I felt I could use the workout and I had nothing else planned that evening.

The yoga instruction was good for my ability, which was moderate at best. Although it was a challenging class for me, I could go at my own pace. I also enjoyed the end of the session when there was a cool-down period for relaxation and meditation. The instructor would circle the room with lavender massage oil in her hands and rub the back of each student's neck. Her touch was pleasant and the music she played was soothing. It was an experience I wanted to repeat.

Each evening when I arrived at the studio, my yoga mat would already be laid out for me next to Noni. After a few sessions, she asked me out for a beer and I obliged. I was seeing a kinder side of the aggressive girl I once knew. The relationship progressed, and Noni became my lover. A month after dating, we flew to Hawaii to visit an old neighborhood friend of mine who grew up across the street from me. He had a diving company in the Kona district of Kailua, Hawaii, and Noni had never visited the aquatic underworld. We had fun in Kona for the most part. The scuba diving was amazing and we toured the island. I remember us hiking down into the Pololu Valley where there was a beautiful black-sand beach. For the first time, we discussed her sister's death in depth.

Noni told me that she had decided to live a better life in memory of her sister. Conversely, she revealed in the same conversation that she purposely went jogging late at night along the dark bike path near the river in Eugene. She hoped that someone would try to attack her. She then would have a reason to fatally hurt someone and do to them what her sister was not able to do. It was a dark mindset.

We were both thirty-five years old when we started dating and neither of us had children. She was living at her grandmother's house, and I was living with my best buddy and golden retriever. She would come over to visit, but it became increasingly difficult to connect. I started noticing traits of the child I once feared and recognized that part of my initial attraction to her was the desire to help a wounded soul. In retrospect, I recognize that my mindset was self-involved. To think that I could change the core of another person was egotistical and naïve. As I grew increasingly reluctant, a poignant event affected me for the worse.

It was a hot spring day, and evening was approaching. I was taking a cool shower when I heard Noni frantically yelling for help outside of the house. Naturally, I shut the water off and ran out to the back yard where the sound was coming from. As I turned out the already opened door I saw her dog latched onto my dog's chest. She was ripping him open with her head down low and her backside high, to leverage her strength in ripping him open further.

I sprinted to the attacking dog, grabbed her with

both hands and threw her away from my dog as far as I could. Instinctively, she lunged back toward my dog to finish him off, and I kicked her away. From there, I picked up my wounded buddy and rushed him over to the back of my hatchback wagon. I set him down gently and then jumped into the driver's seat. Noni asked where I was going, which seemed like an odd question with an obvious answer. I told her that my poor dog needed medical attention and I was taking him to an emergency veterinary hospital.

Noni's initial reaction was to talk me out of leaving and claimed that we could treat my dog by ourselves. This caught me off guard, since it was such an unrealistic solution. I replied to her by asking if she was coming with me. She elected to stay at my house, and I raced off. Time was critical due to my dog's blood loss. He would not have made it without quick medical attention and ultimately was stapled shut from his chest down to his abdomen. The experience was a strong indication that the relationship must end.

There were enough red flags for me to wave my white flag. I invited Noni back to my house to express my feelings that we were better off as friends or even acquaintances. When she arrived, we sat on my back porch and I explained how I felt. I thought she had seen it coming, but her initial reaction suggested otherwise. She curled up into a ball with her head between her knees and started to rock back and forth. When I asked if she was okay, she trembled and moaned.

It felt like she needed some space, so I told her I

would be inside my house. I didn't know what else to do. Later, when I returned outside, she had gained her composure and persuasively proclaimed that she wanted to make our relationship work. My heart sank and I reluctantly agreed to work on it. I felt so badly for her.

Over the next few weeks, Noni purchased five books about relationships, some of which had exercises in them for struggling couples to complete together to help improve their relationship. This was a new concept for me and it felt forced, but I appreciated her initiative. We completed the exercises and learned things about each other that were not helpful. The plan backfired, and our relationship was in further peril. I lost hope for improvement but she would not accept a separation. She recommended I visit her therapist, who would help me understand her better. I agreed to go because I thought it might be a good way to exit the relationship.

The therapist was close to retirement and had her patients come out to her home in the woods, where she had an office. She welcomed me to my session while Noni sat outside the door. The walls felt thin and nothing seemed confidential. It felt like the motive of the session was to persuade me that Noni was capable of having a healthy relationship. I debated her discussion points quietly so Noni would not hear me. I had already checked out of the relationship but I could not stay firm in my decision.

CHAPTER FOUR

# The Gift

As Noni and I continued our daily struggles, a monumental development presented itself. Noni's menstrual cycle was several days late, and each day became more worrisome. One evening after work, she came over to my house with a pregnancy kit. I stood outside the bathroom and awaited the result. There was an uncomfortable silence until I heard Noni yell, "Fuck, Joe!" At that moment, I knew the test result was positive, and we were going to have a child.

Noni stayed over the night of the test and slept in my bed. I lay awake, overcome with emotions, while Noni slept soundly next to me. I was so mixed up. The thought of having a child was exhilarating, while the thought of being with Noni was daunting. I also wondered if she had planned this outcome, having told me before that she could not get pregnant.

We woke up the following morning and went to a local hippie festival, twenty minutes outside of town. Since we already had the tickets, we agreed to go together. I remember being outside the venue, smoking a little marijuana. She wanted to smoke too, but with her being pregnant, it did not seem like a good idea. I expressed my concerns, but she argued that it was not fair that I got to smoke and she could not. She then grabbed the marijuana pipe from me and proceeded to smoke. I felt conflicted and hypocritical but I was not carrying the baby.

Over the next few days, Noni had a chance to absorb this life-changing event. She suggested we marry and she wanted it to happen right away, before she started showing the pregnancy. Although I am not religious, my catholic upbringing had instilled the guilt that I felt about my situation. I also wanted to be involved in my child's life and felt that Noni would make that endeavor difficult for me had I not married her. Six weeks later, we walked through the grass under some old growth black walnut trees and gave our vows. It was a beautiful day and both families were present. It felt like a celebration, but it was also very surreal since everything had happened so fast.

Following the wedding, we purchased a house together in the same neighborhood in which we had grown up. It was a Craftsman-style home that a good friend of mine had just finished building. For the next few months, we built our nest and worked on the relationship through couples' counseling.

The new flavor of therapy was an older gentleman who believed in transparency. There was nothing said that both of us would not hear. However, we ended up discussing trivial matters that did not touch the core of our issues. A popular topic of discussion during our sessions was a picture of a fellow Noni had on her wall at her job. He was a good friend that she had met through work. I was good with that and did not care to know anymore. However, a few days later, we were on a hike and she unexpectedly told me that he was more than a friend. She said that she wanted to be truthful. I was good with that too. But then, for no reason, she decided to elaborate further and divulge their rendezvous. I told her that I would rather leave the past where it belonged.

Her lover was African American, and this became the focal point of our sessions. She claimed that I was prejudiced and jealous that he was dark skinned. The truth was, he could have been orange—her favorite color at the time—and it would have been okay with me. If there was an issue, it was that she kept unwinding her past relationship on me. It was her way to hijack the therapy, avoid the real issues, and play the victim. Our therapy sessions felt like we were back in elementary school, tattling to the teacher. I wondered why we weren't discussing our present difficulties and the baby that was arriving into our lives.

Through the multiple sessions, Noni would wallow in self-pity, and the therapist would act concerned for her. That seemed to be his job. One day, I called the therapist and requested to meet with him alone. He would not agree to meet and told me that I already knew what I needed to do. After that, I asked for a separation. Noni would not accept and insisted on seeing another therapist. She felt that we just had not found the right therapist yet. In her point of view, therapy equaled trying to make the relationship work. The next therapist was a woman who had previously helped a couple that Noni knew. Again, it felt like tattling to the teacher. Each session was convoluted with insignificant rhetoric, rather than focused on the reasons we were not compatible.

Months passed and the birth was near. It felt like I was trying to coexist with an emotional vampire that was sucking the life out of me. I attempted to sleep on my own in the guest room upstairs, and she followed me there. Even though I said I needed space, she would climb into my bed. I could not establish boundaries and felt completely dominated. I remember telling her that I felt bullied by her. From that point forward, I heard that word a lot in therapy. It was Noni who used the word to describe *me*.

Before welcoming our child into the world, Noni and I enrolled in a birthing class. We wanted to be prepared for anything, and if we were not, the midwife and the doula she hired would support us. If that failed, the backup midwife and hospital doctor were standing by. We had our bases more than covered.

It was 2 a.m. on a cold winter morning when Noni went into labor. I called the doula, and she rushed over to our home. She suggested we stay there until the contractions got closer. At the appropriate time, we rushed to the local hospital where Noni remained in labor for many hours. As the contractions got closer, the pain became grueling. Although Noni wanted a natural birth, she asked the midwife for something to block the pain. It was too late for an epidural, so she received fentanyl intravenously. I could not blame her.

After the pain management, Noni would rest between contractions and awaken to push. I saw the crown of the baby and crouched down to his level. I needed to be ready to catch him. What had taken so long up to that point had finally kicked into hyperspeed. The newborn slipped out into my hands and I tearfully rushed him around the bed to where Noni was desperately calling for him. As visitors came to the hospital to meet our new son, they would ask Noni how the birth went. She kept saying, "I did it naturally!" There seemed to be an image to uphold, even if that meant fabricating the image.

It was snowing outside on the day our new family left the hospital. It rarely snowed in the valley, and, to me, this was symbolic of how special my son was in my life. After we arrived back home, there were some sleep-deprived nights for all of us. Each day, I would rise at dawn with my son while Noni slept. Since she nursed him through the night, I would wake up early to take care of him. I had a sling that I would snuggle him into, and we would go for long walks. On our route, we usually stopped by my mother's house for her to see him. To this day, my mother will reminisce about the time we came over to her house and my son's neck was strong enough to support his head. His big blue eyes were glowing and his facial expression was priceless as he stuck his head out of the sling for the first time. It was special for me to share moments like that with my mother.

As the mornings expired, Noni would climb out of bed in a deep depression. Once she started her day, my son became her possession. She explained to me that she was his primary caregiver because he came out of her. She considered me as his secondary caregiver.

CHAPTER FIVE

# Competitive Parenting

Our parenting became very competitive in many ways. Since my son inherited my big head, visitors would comment on our resemblance. For this reason, Noni placed her own baby picture next to his, in the living room, to demonstrate that he looked more like her.

One afternoon, I wanted to go for a walk with my son, but Noni said she would not allow it. Against her words, I put him in the sling anyway and walked out of the house and toward the road. Noni walked out behind me and followed us in silence for the whole walk, about ten paces back. It was our creepiest interaction yet. I finally stopped and asked why she was following us. Pumped with adrenaline, she continued to look straight ahead in silence. Her face was red and her nostrils were flared. Since she did not acknowledge my question, I followed up by asking if she thought I was going to vanish with our baby. Still she did not respond. I continued my walk and ignored Noni as she followed us. When I would stop, she would stop. When I would go, she would go. It was like red light, green light.

Noni had become a danger to me, just as I had felt in my childhood. Even though a separation was inevitable, I made the difficult decision to endure the dysfunction through my son's first birthday. As more time passed, she had fewer boundaries. The more her true colors showed, the less she would try to hide them.

In Noni's opinion, the logical next step for us was to have more therapy. She chose another therapist who previously helped yet another couple she knew. When we attended these sessions we often left my son with the best friend of Noni's deceased sister. In a private conversation with me, the woman mentioned that Noni had always had fight-or-flight tendencies. It was an extremely accurate assessment, and it was one I agreed with.

When we started working with this therapist, my son was almost one-year-old, and my mindset had changed. It was no longer about enduring the relationship. It was about creating an exit strategy and having Noni accept it. I realized, through the help of this therapist, that I had a tendency to try to save the damsel in distress. However, Noni was not a damsel in distress. She was a distressed damsel. It was not situational, but rather who she was.

The therapist explained to me in a private session that Noni displayed behaviors of borderline personality disorder (BPD). I researched BPD and it felt like the resources I read were written about Noni, the very person I feared. The National Alliance of Mental Health states:

> Borderline personality disorder (BPD) is a condition characterized by difficulties in regulating emotion. This difficulty leads to severe, unstable mood swings, impulsivity and instability, poor self-image, and stormy personal relationships. People may make repeated attempts to avoid real or imagined situations of abandonment.

The same periodical mentioned that as many as 5.9 percent of all American adults may suffer from BPD and approximately 75 percent of them are women. It also mentioned that there is no medication specific to treating the core symptoms of BPD (feelings of emptiness, fear of abandonment, and identity disturbance). Psychotherapy is the cornerstone for treatment and improvement. In conversations with the therapist, he said that he could theoretically work with someone with BPD for years and possibly not make any progress.

There is a balance of right and wrong in any healthy relationship, but when someone suffering from BPD feels rejected, the balance is severed. The rejecter represents everything evil, and the person with BPD represents the fight for everything righteous. There is no rationalizing with someone suffering from BPD, because they are not able to get past the rejection. It is like garlic to a vampire.

In our case, feelings of abandonment consistently triggered Noni into fight-or-flight mode. She'd lost sight of my son's best interests and was waging a war. Nothing was amenable and everything was critical. I needed to be a peaceful warrior and to hold firm in my decision to separate and divorce. Otherwise, it would never be accepted by her. We continued to see the therapist, and he continued to work with Noni on accepting the divorce. Once she could not escape the fact that the divorce was really happening, she suggested yet another therapist. It was groundhog day all over again. This time I smartened up and said, "not until I'm moved out." I desperately needed the space.

My search began for an apartment to rent while I continued to pay the mortgage on our home. Noni was not going to leave the house so I could live there and she was unwilling to pay the mortgage. My budget was too tight to support two households, but I had to find a way. My son's first birthday came and went, and we were all still under the same roof. But, I had achieved my goal to make it through his first birthday, as sad as it was. Soon after, our next crisis occurred. It was severe!

I cannot recall what caused the incident but it was probably because I said boys could do something girls couldn't do. Noni was yelling from the bottom of the staircase, and I was upstairs trying to create some space. When I looked down the staircase, I saw her chin raised high and her eyelids fluttering. She was going to let out whatever she was feeling inside whether I wanted to hear it or not. I wanted nothing more than to escape from my own home.

As I walked down the staircase, I had to pass her at the base. She pushed me in the chest and proclaimed, "You're not going anywhere!"

I tried walking to the front door, but she corralled

me with both arms, wrapping them tightly around me. It was a desperate attempt to make me engage and retaliate. I had been through it all before. I pulled my arms into my chest so nothing could be misconstrued.

"Are you going to hold me here forever?" I asked. "Are we going to wither away here together?" Noni continued to hold me firmly, so I stated the obvious. "If it were me doing this to you, it would be a big problem. Please let me go!"

Noni released her grasp and started acting playful. She dug her knuckles into my ribs as if she were tickling me—but twenty times harder. She said, "Come on. Lighten up!"

I asked her to stop prodding me and walked to the back door this time. She had not expected that. As I opened the door, she grabbed my left arm from behind and said, "Don't leave!" I asked her again to let go of me and pulled my arm away. As I walked off the back porch and on to the driveway, she yelled sharply, "You're just freaking out!" and slammed the door.

That same evening, I spoke with another best friend from childhood and asked if he could help me move a few items. His automatic response was, "You just have to work it out, man!" I elaborated on my situation and the incident that had occurred earlier that day. He responded, "I'll be over in the morning." I knew he had better things to do, so his help meant a lot to me.

CHAPTER SIX
# The Split

The next morning, Noni left for class at the University (when her maternity leave had expired, she had quit her full-time job to attend graduate school). My friend came over quickly after she left and helped me pack enough to get through the interim period. I grabbed my clothes, one of the TVs, and the bed from our guest bedroom. From there, we drove a mile away to another best friend's garage and stored the items there. My regret was that I did not grab items that had sentimental value, like my photo albums from childhood and my travels. I never saw those photos again.

After helping me move, my friend invited me, my dog, and my son (when I had him) to stay in the guesthouse located above his detached garage. He was a successful emergency room physician, and his wife was the stay-at-home mother of their two young children. It was the perfect environment for my son. The wife had decorated the vacant guesthouse for us and had inflated a cozy air mattress for the bedroom floor, while my friend had installed an entertainment system.

I was incredibly grateful for their support. They were my family more than my actual family at the time. I'll always feel indebted to them.

After I relocated to the guesthouse, I had to return home to grab my office equipment. I worked from home at the time. Before I headed over, I made the mistake of notifying Noni. She was not at home at the time but rushed there quickly and strategically parked her car behind me to block me in. I was already in my car and had been getting ready to back out of the driveway. She got out of her car like a whirling dervish and stormed over to my vehicle.

There I sat, trapped in the driveway, while Noni ripped opened the doors of my car to find the MacGuffin from an Alfred Hitchcock film. She ransacked my belongings and found an area rug that went under my office chair. As she ripped the carpet out of my vehicle she yelled scornfully, "You bought this after we got married! You're not allowed to take things that are ours!"

After the near cavity search, Noni hopped back in her car and sped off. I was finally free to leave and I drove back to my friend's garage to store my office supplies. It had not occurred to me that I would be followed. After all, I'd seen Noni drive away. Unexpectedly, she pulled up right behind me as I parked in my friend's driveway. I was trapped again.

This time, Noni got out of her car and started yelling at me profusely. I started unloading my car and ignored her the best I could. Her tirade continued, and

I finally acknowledged her by saying, "Leave me alone you psycho!"

She yelled back in fury, "I am not a psycho!"

I immediately regretted saying anything, because her motive had been to get me to engage. Before the situation could escalate any further, I went into my friend's garage and pulled the door down. Noni got back into her car and sped away.

While I stayed at my friend's guesthouse, Noni would not allow me to have any overnight stays with my son. He was like real estate, where possession is nine-tenths of the law. The only way I could see him was at his preschool. I came to realize that I needed legal assistance to exercise my right to have parenting time with my son. I started my search for legal assistance with a business attorney that I knew downtown. He was unwilling to take my case because family law was not his specialty and he felt that cases that involved children were too grueling. He gave me some addresses of local attorneys who specialized in family law, and I walked to the closest one. I figured they all offered the same service, like a mechanic or a doctor. At my destination, I met the attorney. She was a short, stocky East-coast Jewish woman who resembled a bulldog. I thought that was a good sign. Coincidentally, while speaking with her, I learned that we lived in the same neighborhood. We had something in common.

Without doing any research, I hired her.

The American Bar Association states, "As advocate, a lawyer zealously asserts the client's position under the rules of the adversary system." Noni had hired an attorney who worked by this code. She had a win-at-all-cost approach, since she was receiving the directive from Noni (her client). The attorney was also fighting some demons of her own.

During this same period, the opposing attorney's husband, and partner in law, was in legal trouble. He had bought a female minor alcohol right after he had prosecuted her for drinking and driving. His questionable morals and ethics were exposed, and she felt betrayed. The Oregon State Bar reported:

> The disciplinary board approved a stipulation for discipline reprimanding Eugene lawyer [ ] for violating RPC 8.4(a)(2) (commit a criminal act that reflects adversely on the lawyer's honesty, trustworthiness, or fitness as a lawyer in other respects). [Attorney] was the prosecutor for the City of Florence at a hearing in which a minor pled guilty to driving under the influence of intoxicants and entered into a diversion agreement. [Attorney] subsequently contacted the minor, ostensibly for the purpose of checking up on her, and suggested that they meet. [Attorney] drove the minor to a restaurant and purchased two glasses of wine for her in violation of ORS 471.410(2), which prohibits anyone, other than a parent or guardian, from selling, giving, or otherwise making available any alcoholic liquor to a person under the age of 21.

I realized I was dealing with two scorned women. One was a professional in family law, and the other was a seasoned manipulator who wanted nothing more than to alienate me from my child. It was a lethal combination. The saying goes that misery loves company, and they were quite the pair. They would rather have kept me from my child than have allowed me to be an active and supportive father.

Once the divorce proceedings started, we entered a six-month waiting period before the trial. During that time, I wanted to get a temporary parenting plan in place so I could start having overnight stays with my son. Noni insisted (through her attorney) that because she was still breast-feeding, he could not have many overnight stays with me. Her argument was that once he got older we could have more time together, but until that time, he needed more time with her. I ended up agreeing to a temporary parenting plan that offered me much less than fifty percent of the parenting time. My rationalization for accepting the plan was that my son was still breast-feeding, it was temporary, and it was better than no plan. It was also the path of least resistance.

Throughout the waiting period, the opposition's top priority was to intimidate me and tarnish my character. It became clear that our child's best interests were not a common goal. Their approach was about winning, and nothing was out of bounds. Right after the divorce was filed, Noni gave a bag of marijuana her friend had grown (with my name written on the zip lock bag) and a marijuana pipe to her attorney. Her attorney claimed they had my drug paraphernalia.

This was after Noni had smoked marijuana throughout her pregnancy and while she was still nursing. Also, she told me she had grown pot with her mother and stepfather, until they accidentally burned down the operation. No tactic was beneath her, and her strategy was to distort reality. Anything was a potential arrow in her quiver, and everything was free game.

When the exchange of overnight stays began, Noni insisted that we meet in a grocery store parking lot. I recommended the daycare center or one of our homes, but neither was acceptable to her. At each exchange, Noni brought me a thermos of frozen breast milk cubes for me to heat up for my son. She also carried an audio recorder with her and repeatedly said, "I am recording." She would extend her arm out toward me, daring me to say something.

At one point, she got too close to me so I said, "Get that recorder out of my face," and tried removing it from my personal space.

Her response was to dictate into the recorder, "Don't you try to grab my recorder from me!"

Noni was obsessed, desperate, and manic. She did not cope well on the days she was without her son. To hold me responsible for her instability, she insisted that being without her son was more upsetting than her sister's murder. I was anxious for the court-appointed mediation to begin and hoped that it would help us find some resolution.

CHAPTER SEVEN
# A Squandered Solution

The first mediation session became the perfect staging of an ogre and victim scenario. Ever since I had mentioned that I felt bullied by Noni, *bullied* had become a favorite word in her vocabulary. Instead of being the father that wanted to spend time with his child, I became the ogre that bullied her. She was the feeble and defenseless victim. Instead of utilizing the mediation sessions to focus on my son's wellbeing, we exhausted the mediator with he-said-she-said rhetoric. We managed to waste five sessions and made no progress.

A day prior to one of the later sessions, we had another major crisis. Noni asked to come over to the guesthouse for the first time to exchange our son. I initially thought it was better than meeting in the grocery store parking lot, but when she arrived into our living space, she started inspecting the area for child hazards. Every outlet was a child hazard because none had protective covers, and every cabinet was dangerous because none had locks. After the home inspection, she walked outside onto the deck and made herself comfortable in a chair to breast feed. She evidently was not ready to leave, so I got her a blanket to keep them warm. As she sat outside for what seemed like forever, I sat inside doing office work.

Once Noni decided she was ready to leave with my son, I walked outside and accompanied them to her car. She buckled my son into the back seat, and I leaned into the opened door to hug him goodbye. As I leaned in, Noni flipped a switch again and said abruptly, "Get out! You already said goodbye." Then she shifted her car into reverse and pressed on the gas. My feet were on the pavement, and my body was still in the car. In my business suit and dress shoes, I started running sideways and backwards. Since I was pinned in the door frame, I could not afford to stumble.

As I was trying to keep my feet under me, Noni abruptly slammed on the brakes, jumped out of the car, and ran up to my friend's house. She started ringing the doorbell repeatedly, and my friend's wife opened the door. She slipped into the house and shut the door behind her quickly. My son and I watched this from the car. I unbuckled him from his seat and walked with him up to the house.

As I walked in the door with my son in my arms, I heard Noni beg my friend's wife, "Can you come outside? We are having a difficult time!" Luckily for me, my friend's wife was familiar with her erratic behavior already. A few days earlier, my son had contracted hand, foot, and mouth disease, and my physician friend confirmed the diagnosis. When I notified Noni, she became hysterical. She instantly called my physician friend and scornfully reprimanded him, saying that he was not allowed to medically diagnose our child. "He is allergic to amoxicillin!" she exclaimed, even though my friend had not prescribed him any medication.

My friend's wife called her bluff and refused to get involved. Once she recognized that her ploy was not working, Noni ripped our child out of my arms and stormed out the front door. My son was startled, frightened, and crying. It was obvious that he could feel her intense emotions. I walked out of the house and followed my son and Noni from a distance. I was worried about my son and fearful of the hands he was in, but the situation was out of my control. All I could do was watch.

Once they were both in the car and the car was running, I waved good-bye to my son. My wave triggered Noni and she leapt back out of the car and bull rushed me, screaming. Because she was coming straight at me, I put my hands on my quadriceps and stabilized my core. She slammed into me as hard as she could while I braced and remained stable. She bounced off me, gave another loud scream, and stormed back to her car. As she backed out of my friend's driveway, she rolled down her window and yelled at me with conviction, "You really blew it this time!" Then she sped off.

The next day at mediation, Noni arrived first to instill her influence. She requested that we be placed in separate rooms and that she meet first with the mediator. After their discussion, the mediator came to the room where I was waiting. She asked, "What happened yesterday? She is really scared in there!" I implored the mediator to recognize what was really happening. I asked her to see through the frantic behavior, and I think she did. Even so, after five sessions of mediation, nothing had been accomplished.

CHAPTER EIGHT

# The Settlement

Both the custody hearing and the financial settlement hearing dates were looming, and Noni and I had not agreed on anything. Months had passed and our attorneys had not been in communication. I thought the silence between them was peculiar, since we should have been able to settle amicably and move on with our lives.

One day, I visited the old neighborhood to see my mother and decided to drive by the house I once lived in (and still paid for). As I drove by, I noticed there were no toys in the yard, so I pulled over to take a closer look and walked up to the porch. When I looked inside the living room window, I saw that the house had been ransacked. Since I still had the house key on my key chain, I unlocked the front door to investigate further. When I walked in, I saw that everything was gone. Only garbage, dog hair, and dirt remained. My initial reaction was to contact my attorney and ask if I could move back into my home. She said that I should do it quickly and change the locks. My son and I had been sleeping on an air mattress at my friend's guesthouse for a few months, so it would feel good to be back home. It would also help my son feel more grounded.

Noni had relocated weeks before my discovery. She had wanted to be closer to the university campus and had also wanted to keep me displaced. When she discovered that I had moved back into the house, she lied to her attorney about a verbal agreement we supposedly had about the house. The alleged agreement was that neither of us would live in the house and that we would sell it. I ended up staying in the house, but at a large cost.

The day before the custody trial, our attorneys communicated, and there was an offer on the table. It was to maintain the temporary parenting plan and to settle on a modified joint-custody arrangement. I did not know what this meant, but it sounded better than sole custody.

In the modified joint-custody scenario, one parent (Noni) would have the final custodial decision-making authority on matters that could not be agreed upon. In essence, it was a sole-custody arrangement. The only difference was, if needed, it would be easier to go back to court regarding custody. My attorney recommended that I should accept the offer and said that I could do worse in court. I took her advice and accepted the heavily weighted offer that gave me less parenting time and no custodial decision-making authority. It was a workaround by the opposition to get their desired result.

Regarding the financial settlement, I had previously asked Noni what she felt would be fair compensation for child support and for removing her from the deed of our home. Her response was that she wanted spousal support, as well as child support. The amount she wanted was absurd, at three times the amount of the recommended state child support calculator. All that support for a dysfunctional marriage that lasted less than two years.

After multiple attempts to negotiate, I remember being on the phone with Noni just days before the settlement deadline. We discussed her payout on our house, which had lost significant value due to the market crash. She was unrealistic and demanded thirty thousand dollars in addition to her original investment in the down payment. Her argument was that my son deserved to live in a house that she owned, but she could not afford a down payment. She claimed that renting a residence would be an unstable environment for my son because they could potentially have to move at any moment.

I tried negotiating something reasonable with an unreasonable person. I was willing to take the hit on the devaluation and pay her back what she put in. After extensive negotiating over the phone, she said she would accept eighteen thousand dollars beyond her initial investment. Even though she had never made a mortgage payment, this agreement was the path of least resistance again and meant that I could avoid the stress of court. It was a stellar financial return for her in a down real estate market. Instead of being rational, she had been a shrewd businesswoman.

The following day, my attorney called to inform me that she had spoken with the opposing attorney. They had discussed our verbal settlement, and the eighteen thousand dollars we had agreed on had grown to twenty thousand, overnight. Noni had welched on our agreement. When I told my attorney that we had agreed on eighteen thousand, she said, "So what's another two thousand dollars? It's better than going to court!" When I challenged her poor advice and explained the principle of it, she sharply replied, "Hey, I wasn't the one that fucked her!" It was apparent that I did not have an ally in my attorney. Against my better judgement, I continued on the path of least resistance and agreed to pay the inflated amount on the house. I also agreed to pay two hundred dollars more a month in child support than what the state child support calculator recommended. Spousal support was not part of the settlement.

I wanted to put Noni and the fraternity of attorneys behind me. Even though Noni's attorney had squeezed more money out of me, I consoled myself that it would help her move closer to stability. I also presumed the funds would go toward my child's upbringing.

## CHAPTER NINE
# The Web

My son's second birthday arrived soon after our financial settlement. Noni had him for that day, and I had him for the night. I had planned a birthday party at my house for him and invited friends and family to celebrate the occasion. The party started an hour before the exchange so everyone would already be there when I picked him up. We were all excited to see him!

While my guests stayed back and socialized, my sister and I went to pick up my son at the grocery store parking lot. I had my sister come along because I thought it would decrease the chance of an altercation. Unluckily for my son, it was to no avail. When I picked him up, Noni had already sedated him with Benadryl. She insisted that he hadn't been feeling well, and so she had given him the Benadryl fifteen minutes before our exchange. I did not respond, so she approached my sister and repeated herself. After her blatant confession, she handed my son over to me.

I turned away from her and toward my car to go

buckle him in the back seat. As I leaned into the car, she grabbed my shoulder from behind and pulled me back forcefully. "I want to say goodbye to him again!" she exclaimed. I asked her not to grab me and handed my son back over to her before she became more desperate. She hugged him sorrowfully, as if she might never see him again. When she handed him to me the second time, I rushed for the car and buckled him in. I wanted to get out of the parking lot before anything else could happen. Once we got back home, my son was unable to stay awake for his own birthday party due to the sedation.

After my son's second birthday came his second annual medical exam. He had a female pediatrician who worked very well with him. Because I was attending the exam, Noni made an example of me. She barraged the physician with very basic questions, insinuating that I was not caring well for my son.

"How many times a day should his teeth be brushed? How many pieces of candy per day should he have? How many hours a night should he sleep? What are appropriate shows he should be watching?"

I asked her why she was peppering the pediatrician with common-sense questions and she disturbingly responded, "I am asking my son's doctor questions about my son!"

As the pediatrician left the examination room to get a vaccine for my son, I walked out behind her. I did not want to risk being alone in the same room as Noni. She had already tried to paint a distorted picture of me with the pediatrician, and it would have been negligent of me to allow her an opportunity to create a bigger scene. I walked out of the examination room, and the door shut behind me.

The pediatrician faced me in the hallway and said, "I'm really sorry!" Before I could say anything in return, Noni opened the examination room door, stood in the doorway, and bullishly denied us the courtesy of confidentiality. So that we could talk in private, the pediatrician walked back over to the door and shut it again. As the pediatrician walked back over to me, Noni opened the door again. It was a battle of wills, and my paranoid ex-wife won. There was too much at stake for her to allow the pediatrician and me to speak in confidence. I ended up shaking my head in frustration and leaving the clinic.

The next day I called the pediatrician and we had a candid conversation. We both agreed that it would be best for my son if I did not attend future appointments. Though it was exactly what Noni had wanted, it was the best thing for my son. The pediatrician promised me that she would notify me firsthand of any significant healthcare developments.

As my son grew from a toddler to a little boy, there continued to be outside influences, and noninfluences, monitoring our lives. One noninfluence was a private mediation service that I hired and that Noni agreed to attend with me. She got to feel engaged again.

My objective for mediation was to establish a more balanced parenting plan. There were too many back-and-forth exchanges with our son (six in a two-week period), and I wanted him to have a chance to feel more grounded. At the end of each session, Noni said she would consider my requests for fewer exchanges and more parenting time. But when the next session came around, she had reconsidered them. Five more sessions were consumed, and there was no progress.

A potential negative influence for my son and I was the preschool he attended. Noni befriended one of the administrators, whom she utilized to alienate me from my son. She convinced the woman that my visits to the preschool were negatively affecting my son's daily routine and that they needed to stop. Since I worked from home, I would let my son sleep in on my parenting days and take him to the preschool when he was fully rested. Sometimes, on the days I did not have him, I would pick him up to go have lunch at a Korean restaurant down the street. He loved the teriyaki chicken! This was our routine, and Noni did not like it, because it allowed us more bonding time on her parenting days. It felt like we were back in the sand box at elementary school again.

Noni and the preschool administrator planned a meeting to discuss restricting my visits to the preschool. Noni, the preschool administrator, my son's preschool teacher, and my son's child psychologist, who I had never met, were in the conference room when I arrived. A few days prior to the meeting, I had a hint that something was transpiring when I visited my son at the preschool and he said, "You can't be here dad or you will get arrested. Dad, what does arrested mean?" It broke my heart!

My son's child psychologist proved to be a positive influence for my son and me. He was a distinguished older gentleman with a PhD in psychology and was known by his peers for his leadership in child advocacy in traumatic cases. An example of his work was the extensive care he gave to the surviving children of Diane Downs, a renowned psychopath in the early 1980s who shot her three children, killing one, and was the subject of "Small Sacrifices" by Ann Rule. From there, his services were utilized in many tragic cases. The most recent one I'm aware of is the Amanda Stott-Smith case, where a woman threw both of her children off the Sellwood Bridge in Portland. Only one child survived. The psychologist was compassionate and dedicated to the wellbeing of children.

When the meeting started, Noni and the preschool administrator said they wanted to implement some rules. I was told that I needed to have my son at the preschool by 8:30 a.m., and that I could not pick him up until 2:00 p.m. on my parenting days. I was also no longer allowed to take my son out to lunch on my nonparenting days. My response to the collaborators was that I was merely trying to be involved in my child's life. I was part of the solution and not part of the problem, I explained. After the administrator expressed her concerns about the importance of routine, the child psychologist spoke up.

He started by comparing humans to a pride of lions and discussing our common primal instincts. He said my son benefitted greatly from my visits. Having male support in his pride gave him the ability to feel an instinctual connection with me. The psychologist also suggested my son sleep in, to feel fully rested. He was a growing boy who required ample sleep. The last point the psychologist made was that my son benefitted more by being in my care than he would by spending time at preschool. Noni and her ally remained quiet, but Noni requested a follow-up meeting for one month later.

At the second meeting, I walked into the same conference room and saw the same people—except the psychologist. The meeting started when Noni said that she was only comfortable with my son going to lunch with me once a week. This time it was my son's teacher who came to my defense and said that there were no apparent issues with the current arrangement. The open-door policy would remain. I was welcome to visit anytime and take my son to lunch. The meeting ended abruptly and I was thankful.

I remained proactive in my attempt to improve my son's parenting schedule and asked Noni if she would consider other mediation. She agreed again, but wanted to go back to the court-appointed mediator we visited the first time around. When I called the mediator's office, she explained that to see her again, we would need to file for a modification of parenting time through the court. Noni agreed to move forward, and I filed the modification to receive the sessions.

By now, the mediator knew us both well. In the first session, I requested to meet in separate rooms; otherwise, there would be too many diversions. By the third session, the mediator held Noni accountable. She told her that if she wanted to continue mediation, she had to be willing to agree on something.

Noni felt blocked in and decided to take a different course of action. She forfeited the remaining mediation appointments and requested a custody evaluation through our attorneys. She was no longer interested in considering compromises and she wanted the permanent title of sole custodial parent. Mediation had unexpectedly become a negative influence. Also during this round of mediation, I had started dating a woman, and the relationship was getting serious. Noni told the mediator that I had said to my son that my girlfriend was his new mother, which I never said. I wondered if the threat of another woman was partly the reason for the proposed custody evaluation.

I recall taking my girlfriend to the beach with her son and my son. We were going to be late getting home, and I had emailed, texted, and called Noni to let her know. After receiving my messages, she had rushed down to the police station and called me from inside the station. She left a voice message saying that she was at the police station and that there was a warrant out for my arrest. I also received a voice message from a police officer who calmly explained that our parenting plan was a court document, signed by a judge, and that it must be followed. In his message, the officer gave me the option to call him back.

Because Noni had said there was a warrant for my

arrest, I called the officer back. The officer answered and explained to me that it was a civil matter and that Noni had asked him to call me. There had been no warrant issued for my arrest.

## CHAPTER TEN
# The Hired Gun

The proposed custody evaluation became a pressing issue, and I needed to respond to the request. I retained the same attorney as before because the opposing attorney had contacted her with the request. I also had some retainer funds still available.

At first, I did not agree to participate in the custody evaluation because I knew the cards would be stacked against me. But the opposing attorney came back and said that her client would pay for the evaluation. It was clear that Noni saw it as a good investment. She could have permanent control of the major decisions regarding my son and solidify her title of sole custodial parent.

My attorney explained that Noni could simply enforce the custody evaluation through the court, and she suggested that I should take her offer. She also suggested that I could win custody since Noni was, in her words, a *whack job*. I hesitantly took my attorney's advice and agreed to participate in the custody evaluation.

Before the custody evaluation began, my attorney told me to take good notes on the questions the evaluator would ask. She said she wanted to know for the sake of future clients. It was clear to me that I would not get any preparation from my attorney. Also, there were no consequences on her end. She was going to get paid, regardless. But on my end, the consequences were significant and permanent.

The opposing attorney selected the custody evaluator, and there were no objections from my representation. He was an older man from a small conservative town south of Eugene, and his educational background was in social work. I did not feel that he was qualified to decide my son's fate.

Before I discuss the custody evaluation boondoggle, I want to share some front-end learning opportunities. To learn them on the back end of an evaluation is devastating:

- The custody evaluation is a zero-sum game. To the most persuasive party belong the spoils, to the less persuasive party, the fruits of discrimination.
- The custody evaluator is not legally capable of recommending joint custody.
- The custody evaluator is not required to have a degree in child psychology or child development.
- The custody evaluator can also negatively affect parenting time schedules through his or her recommendation.
- Sole custody is permanent unless the non-custodial parent is able to establish a signifi-

cant and unanticipated change of circumstance, such as drug addiction, child abuse, psychiatric instability, or relocation out of the area.
- A person with a personality disorder can outwit a custody evaluation.

As an analogy, a custody evaluation is like a snapshot taken with a filtered lens in a circus tent. The evaluator gets a still-print view of a distorted reality, where everything is off-color. In the evaluator's defense, I believe it is impossible to reach a decision in the best interests of the child. He or she has been given an altered sample of fantasy and the decision is a Hobson's Choice: sole custody or nothing.

An analogy for a more effective custody evaluation is a biographical documentary film with extensive character development and a predictable ending. An evaluation is a critical decision that requires time to understand the characters, due diligence to understand the scenario, and the tools to make the best recommendation for the child.

The last analogy I'll suggest is the most effective. A custody evaluation should be like a silent film with mimes, because this type of film no longer exists and neither should custody evaluations. There are better solutions that will be covered later in the book.

In my case, the custody evaluator reached his decision by reviewing our written testimonies, administering abbreviated personality tests, conducting two personal interviews (one with my son), and completing phone interviews with character references.

To kick off the custody evaluation, the evaluator required written testimonies and lists on the following topics:
- A timeline of events in my life.
- My concerns about the other parent.
- Reasons why having me as the sole custodial parent is in my child's best interest.
- A contact list of nonfamily personal references.
- A contact list of collateral references.

Once I finished my written testimonies and lists, my attorney wanted to meet and read them before I mailed them off to the evaluator. She wanted to check for grammatical errors because, she explained, she used to be an English teacher. After the hour-long English lesson, I passed the test and sent off the information.

There remained two personal interviews with the custody evaluator and phone interviews with some of our character and collateral references. The first personal interview was between me and the evaluator and held at my house. We discussed the information I had mailed to him. The custody evaluator said that he was amazed because Noni wrote the same concerns about me.

I elaborated on Noni's physical aggression and stalking behaviors. When I mentioned that she followed us on walks the custody evaluator replied, "Like a robot!" I also mentioned that Noni was still breastfeeding, sleeping, and showering with my son. He was turning five years old, I emphasized. I thought the reality of the situation would speak for itself, but the custody evaluator responded by saying, "She said she is weaning him."

The bias I felt from the evaluator was apparent, so I mentioned a 2009 United States Census Bureau statistic to him. It indicated that approximately 82 percent of all sole custodial parents were women. His response to me was that before the industrial period, men had all the parental power and rights. He evaded my concerns about the blatant bias that was present.

The second interview was again at my house, but this time my son was with me. The custody evaluator wanted to observe our dynamic and assess our relationship. At first, we played Go Fish. Then, we got out two foam swords for interactive play. Sword fighting was my son's favorite activity at the time. We engaged in our duel, and my son shouted, "Tell it to the judge!" as he playfully brought on the onslaught. It was something he had heard on the television, and he was showing off for the custody evaluator.

The custody evaluator psychoanalyzed the activity and my son's behavior. He indicated he was concerned about the aggression my son displayed and the words of litigation he used. From my point of view, my little boy had been rough housing with his father and thoroughly enjoying it.

After the extreme interactivity, the custody evaluator had me complete an abbreviated personality test while he spent time with my son. The Minnesota Multiphasic Personality Inventory test (MMPI-2) is the typical personality test used to assess personality traits and psychopathology. It consists of 567 true or false questions. The personality test Noni and I completed was the Personality Assessment Inventory (PAI) with 344 questions, and it seemed far less effective. It felt like the custody evaluator was groomed for this evaluation.

At the end of the second interview, the evaluator said that Noni recognized that my son would need more time in my care in the future, but for now, she felt that he needed a primary residence and caregiver. It was her way of coming across as reasonable to get the desired result. She knew that there would not be any custody checkpoints in the future. The evaluators decision would be permanent!

When the interviews were completed, I did not feel good about my chances. Would he believe the big ogre who already had his child for less parenting time, or would he believe the frail victim who hired his services and was still breastfeeding? We spent very little of the time discussing the wellbeing of my son and most of the time discussing how Noni and I couldn't play nice in the sandbox. In reality, the forum was about discrediting the other parent. Once the custody evaluator had finished his work, a meeting was scheduled to receive his recommendation.

My attorney and I walked to the meeting, which was held in a conference room at the opposing firm. On the way, my attorney mentioned that the opposing attorney had recently recruited her to work for her firm. It felt like a strong conflict of interest. When we entered the conference room, Noni was already sitting down with the custody evaluator and her attorney.

There was a quick reintroduction of everyone, and then the custody evaluator took the floor. He started by explaining the devastation one of us might feel due to his decision, then he rolled out his recommendation. It was no surprise that he recommended that Noni be the sole custodial parent. He also recommended that we have bigger blocks of parenting time moving forward, but even less of that time would be in my care.

The outcome of the evaluation was worse than I had imagined. Noni was ecstatic, and her attorney was proud of her accomplishment. When the evaluator asked if we had any questions, I asked him, "What could I have done differently?" My question was broad, and he did not answer.

When I exited the building with my attorney, she told me that she had never had anyone ask that question of a custody evaluator before. She was appalled that I had questioned the social worker whose recommendation negatively impacted my relationship with my son. She also advised me to accept the evaluator's recommendation. She said that if I did not, Noni could enforce it through the court.

I was so deflated; I did not have the mindset to defend myself. My attorney had not been my advocate and the cards had been stacked against me. I accepted the recommendation and lost the fight I had wanted no part of. Later, I was told by many sources that I should have never agreed to the custody evaluation, that I should have resisted, unless it had been mandated by the court. From my experience, I would agree with that advice, especially since my son had been so young, which played in Noni's favor.

After the custody evaluation and English lesson, my retainer balance with my attorney was in the red. I received a call from her with the notification. She said that I owed her $500 and that I needed to pay her right away. Her exact words were, "Where's my money Joe?" She was my attorney, English teacher, and debt collector.

## CHAPTER ELEVEN
# Bouncing Back

Following the custody evaluation, I was emotionally wounded and needed to recover from the effect the evaluation had on me. I had been stripped of my rights as a father, and I had lost more time with my son. I sank into a heavy depression. It was critical that I dust myself off to be present and emotionally available for my son.

The couples' counselor who had educated me on BPD and helped me through the separation was now my shaman. He had studied Eastern philosophy in India and had learned self-healing techniques, which he shared with me. He helped me work through my feelings of hopelessness and sense of loss from the evaluation.

Parenting is a marathon, and I was sprinting in my mind. The counselor helped me put things into perspective and reminded me that parenting was a lifelong endeavor. Noni would not always have control over his destiny. He explained to me, "Just as the sun rises from the East and sets in the West, tyrants will always become victims of their own tyranny." To me, this meant that things would change someday, and I would have more input and time with my son. It somehow helped me feel more optimistic about the future and reminded me that losing custody was not a death sentence.

Part of my sadness was from the disappointment I felt in myself. I had accepted the custody evaluator's recommendation instead of going to court. I felt I should have fought harder and disputed the recommendation before a judge. But the counselor reminded me that the decisions I made in the past were the best decisions I could have made with the information I had. It was a natural response to beat myself up and dwell on what I could have done differently, but it was not realistic. When I blamed myself for the outcome, the counselor would say to me, "You can't be where you're not." The present was the only reality that truly existed.

The counselor informed me that there were three forms of thought and communication: the adult, the parent, and the child. The adult represented rational thought and logic. The parent represented reprimands and could haves, should haves, and would haves. The child represented the loss, hopelessness, and self-pity I felt. My mindset was in the parent form, and I was scolding my inner child.

A milestone in my recovery was when the counselor asked me to explain how I was feeling. My response to him was that I felt misjudged and extremely frustrated. He explained that there was one thing stronger than the frustration I felt. It was the want. I did not understand the lesson yet, so he expanded by asking me if I wanted more time with my son. I teared up and said yes. He followed by asking me if I wanted Noni to treat me like an equal parent and with respect. I confirmed again, yes. Then he explained that the frustration I felt was due to that want. Once I recognized that the want was out of my control, the frustration I felt would subside.

The counselor also taught me that my mind was a wonderful servant, but it made a horrible leader. If I learned to control my mind, to help myself heal with positive and optimistic thought, I would be enlightened. But, if I let my mind control me through dwelling on the past or worrying about the future, I would spiral downward. Throughout my struggles, the counselor constantly reminded me, "You have to do the work!"

I was also restless and could not sleep at night from the sadness and anxiety I felt. The counselor taught me to meditate, which was a new concept for me. The mantra he taught me was Om Namah Shivaya. It translates to, "I bow to my inner self." When I said the words aloud, or quietly in my mind, I absorbed the self-respect, love, and forgiveness implied in the mantra. It helped me feel inner peace and to recognize that my actions were noble. When I could not sleep at night, this mantra would slip me into dreamland with the self-respect and dignity I deserved.

Exercise was also critical for my recovery. The endorphins helped my mood, and exerting myself helped my mind rest. Exercise helped me get back to the basics and appreciate what I had: my health! When

I would go running, I would focus on my breathing patterns, the sounds of the river, the smells of the rain, and the beautiful sights of the natural environment around me. Since I had lost my appetite, the exercise also helped me to get it back and to eat nutritious food. It also helped me feel more rested at night so I could sleep better. The exercise, nutrition, and sleep were critical to my recovery.

A good friend also helped me put things into perspective. He said, "It's a bummer what happened. But, you know that you still have it better than most people around the world, right?" It reminded me of the saying in Brazil, "Chorando com barriga cheia!" which translates to, "Crying with a full belly!" If I had food in my stomach, I was doing better than many people. Besides having my health and food in my belly, I had a roof over my head and a beautiful son to guide. There was a lot to be thankful for! It was high time to stop feeling sorry for myself and to be grateful for what I had.

CHAPTER TWELVE

# Finding Time

Since I had even less time with my son, I made our time together count more than ever! Additionally, I became very resourceful in finding extra time with him. Like his preschool, the elementary school my son attended had an open-door policy for parents. If I was not traveling for work, I would usually visit my son at lunchtime on my nonparenting days. His lunchtime was only twenty minutes long, but it gave us the opportunity to check in and connect.

Visiting my son at school was also the only way I could know how he was doing on the days I did not have him. Noni would not answer my phone calls or give him my voice messages. Since he started grade school, I have also given my son three cell phones. Each one of them has been confiscated by his mother. Instead of allowing him the comfort of hearing from me, Noni considered our communication competitive in nature and obstructed it in any way that she could.

Another great way I stayed involved was to volunteer at school events and field trips. It gave me a chance to spend more time with my son and to get to know his classmates. It also gave the school a chance to get to know me. Noni preferred that I was not involved and played the martyr role with his school. Before one field trip, she coerced my son's homeroom teacher into emailing me to ask that I not attend. I had attended the last field trip, so Noni felt it was her turn. I graciously told the teacher that my time was limited with my son, that he wanted me there, and that I would be attending.

Coaching has been another valuable way to be involved in my son's life. It has given me the ability to play an active role in his development firsthand. I have coached kids since I was a teenager, so it has been a great fit. The dividends for me are that I have gotten to see him more, and he has felt a sense of pride with his peers.

Taking advantage of my son's school vacation time has led to some of our best bonding experiences. I am an avid world traveler and have traveled to five continents. However, I am unable to take my son out of the country because Noni will not share his passport. In lieu of international travel, we have gone snorkeling with manta rays and dolphins in Hawaii and fished with grizzly bears in Alaska, and we have taken many road trips.

One memorable road trip was during spring break when we drove down to Disneyland. We had planned to fly down, but we could not get an available flight back in time for the parenting exchange. Noni would not allow us to arrive home late, so we hopped in my car and drove south to the destination. It was an amazing adventure that neither of us will forget, and we made it home in time for the exchange.

Noni has been fortunate to have his passport. She has been able to take him anywhere she wanted, with no one to ask. In fact, they traveled to Costa Rica a few years back during summer break. My son called me two days before they were coming home, and I asked him how he was doing. His response was, "Pretty good. I get to come home in two days to see you!"

It has been disappointing that Noni has not been willing to let him share new international cultural experiences with me. This has only deprived him of extraordinary life experiences. One of the last international trips I asked to take him on was to the 2014 World Cup in Brazil. Noni said that she was not comfortable with the possible danger the trip represented for him. As a consolation, she found a news clip of a public political protest in Brazil. It was a peaceful demonstration against the government for spending too much money on the stadiums being built. This was used as proof to my son that his mother had made the best decision for his wellbeing.

Meanwhile, I went to the World Cup and missed some parenting days with my son. Before I left on the trip, I tried exchanging some parenting days, but Noni was not amenable. It was a once-in-a-lifetime experience for me to visit my Rotary Exchange host family and to go to World Cup soccer matches in the same trip. I did not want to miss the opportunity, and I forfeited the parenting days. My son still reminds me of the days that we lost and holds me accountable. It means a lot to me, how much he values our time together.

The most drastic and effective way I found to be more involved in my son's life was to move across town, nearer to his school and Noni's house. I used to drive thirty minutes, roundtrip, to see him. There was a lot of windshield time spent driving back and forth, and it made sense to relocate. Now I can coast down the hill—less than a mile—and be at his school.

CHAPTER THIRTEEN
# The Bitter Truth

While I was creating ways to stay involved in my son's life, Noni continued to take him to the child psychologist. She seemed dependent on therapy, and it made her look good on paper. I was not invited to the sessions, so I made my own appointments with the psychologist. My original impression of the psychologist (from the meeting at the preschool) was that he had my son's best interests in mind. He had already helped my son and I at the preschool, because he recognized the importance of my involvement in my son's life. Without the psychologist, I would have been ostracized.

I met with the psychologist periodically, and sometimes I would bring my son to the sessions, per the psychologist's request. He wanted to evaluate our interactions and observe our relationship. It was safe to roughhouse like lions and demonstrate our real connection. The consistent feedback I received from the psychologist in our sessions was that my son desperately wanted more time with me.

Since the psychologist, Noni, and I were all aware of how my son felt, I requested a joint psychology session with just Noni. She agreed to attend, because it gave her a forum to exercise her victimization, domination, and control.

The session was a textbook example of past dysfunctional therapy sessions that had only led to chaos. I mentioned that my son wanted more time with me, and that I also wanted more time with him. Noni responded by saying that I needed to be nice to her for two years before she would consider allowing us more time together. I explained to Noni that my request was also my son's request. He wanted to spend more time with me, and it would help him feel more content and grounded. The request was about my son's wellbeing and not her need to dominate me further. However, the rejection she felt from the divorce was too strong, and the control she had been given as the sole custodial parent was too powerful. She could not resist misusing her power, once again. After I had explained to Noni that my request was not about her, she felt cornered.

Predictably, her reaction was to hijack the session. She trembled and stared into space and claimed that she did not do well with people yelling at her. However, my voice was not raised, and I was merely holding her accountable for not considering my son's best interests. The psychologist looked at Noni with concern. As he looked in her direction, she pointed over at me and claimed, "He just said fuck you to me!" The psychologist turned his head in my direction, in confusion. We were both confused, but I caught on quickly. It was her technique of relieving herself from accountability by sabotaging the real discussion. The session had ended in chaos, and my request had been denied.

In the following session with the psychologist, I explained that I was concerned with my son's emotional wellbeing. I wanted to protect him, but how could I protect him from his mother? The behaviors she displayed were not isolated to me. My son also felt the brunt of her instability, and it was affecting him emotionally. The psychologist explained that his job as my son's therapist was to support him and to keep his best interests in mind. He needed to remain biased toward his patient and nonbiased regarding his patient's parents. Since my son was adamant about spending more time in my care, the psychologist agreed to work with Noni to help her accept my involvement.

Months passed, and my son started a new year of grade school. On the first day that I got to pick him up, I noticed Noni's last name written on his school folder. When I opened the folder, Noni's last name was on all his paperwork. I walked to the front office and inquired why her last name was being used instead of mine. The front office staff person said that Noni indicated that although his legal last name was mine, he went by her last name now.

At risk of adding to the chaos that seemed to follow us, I escalated the issue with the school principal. My son should not feel conflicted or be confused about his last name. When I expressed my concern to the principal, he said that he would need to seek legal counsel from the school district. Since she was the sole custodial parent, he was not sure if she had the right to change his last name with the school. I told the principal that if his legal counsel said that it was okay for Noni to change his last name on him, then I would want to speak with his legal counsel because that decision would be unacceptable. A few days later the principal tracked me down in the hallway near the front office. He said that the school had rectified the situation and that my son had my last name again.

The holiday season arrived a few months later. I was helping coach my son's basketball team, so I got to see him more often. On the last practice before the holiday break, my son and his mother gave me a wrapped gift. I thought it would be nice to open it at Christmas with my son, so I brought it home and placed it under the Christmas tree. When the time arrived for me to have my son for holiday, I finally got to open his gift. There were two items inside the box. One was a bright red sucker in the shape of puckered hot lips, and the other was a pile of fake poop. After I opened the gift, my son said, "Isn't that funny dad!" I swallowed my humiliation and agreed that it was funny for my son's sake. Then, I let him eat the sucker.

My son's desire to spend more time in my care continued to manifest. One day, there was no school, and the exchange with Noni took place at my house. When she arrived in the driveway, I walked him outside and hugged him goodbye. He said that he did not want to leave, and he asked me if he could stay longer. I told him that it was okay with me if it was okay with his mother. He walked over to the driver side window of Noni's car and asked her the question. Noni declined his request and told him to get in her car. As he pleaded with her, she got out of her car and wrapped her arms around him like she was trying to be compassionate. Once she got hold of him, she tried stuffing him into her car.

My son squirmed out from under Noni's grasp to escape her clutch. From there, he sprinted past me in the driveway and ran back into the house through the back door. Once he was inside the house, he ran up the stairs and into the bathroom, where he locked himself in. I followed behind him into the house and walked up the stairs, but he would not let me into the bathroom. We were at a stalemate, and I was in a tough position. I did not want to force my son to leave against his will, and I did not want to be negligent with Noni.

Meanwhile, Noni had stomped up to the front porch of my house and started ringing the doorbell like it was Space Invaders. Then, she called my eighty-year-old mother and tattled on me for something that was out of my control. She blamed me for the situation, as if I was the master mind of the mutiny. She was unwilling to look within herself to understand why he did not want to go with her. She had a maniacal way of distorting reality to play into her favor. I was not going to force my son out of the bathroom and make him leave with his livid mother. I also was not comfortable with going outside to reason with an unreasonable person. Anything could happen, and it would be her word against mine. I did not like those odds.

After assessing the unfortunate situation, I recognized that I needed third party intervention. Something I had never done before was call the police for assistance, and this was the first time. After explaining my predicament to the dispatcher, she said that it was not a police matter. It was a civil matter, and there was nothing she could do for me. She suggested that I contact the local crisis intervention center. I took the police dispatcher's advice and contacted the center.

Twenty minutes later, a team of two individuals arrived at my house, and I invited them inside. Noni had relocated to her car. My son had finally come out of the bathroom but would still not go outside, thinking of the trouble he was in. The team interviewed my son and asked him why he did not want to go with his mother. He said that he feared the trouble he had gotten himself into, and he was afraid to go with her.

Following the interview with my son, the crisis intervention team walked outside to Noni's car to speak with her. They told her that he was afraid to go with her because of the trouble he'd gotten himself into and asked her to come back one hour later. They also requested that she not punish my son when she got him to her house. She agreed to both of their requests. Then the team members came back into my house and asked my son if he would be willing to go with his mother in one hour's time. They also promised him that she would not punish him. My son agreed to the arrangement, even though he was terrified. He had to go with her, and I could not protect him. Once the agreement was established, the crisis intervention team left my house.

Noni came back to my house exactly one hour later. My son kept his promise to go home with her, and Noni kept her promise not punish him that day. Instead, she waited until the following day and grounded him to his room for the day. It was a loophole in the agreement. She was able to keep her promise and still punish him for his insubordination.

It was evident that I needed to seek legal representation to advocate for my son. He was six years old and did not have a voice in the court of law. I could sense his dire frustration, and I could not make any progress with Noni through mediation, therapy, or direct communication. I would never forgive myself if I witnessed my son's suffering without trying to help him in every way that I could.

CHAPTER FOURTEEN

# The Last Resort

Court was the last resort to secure more parenting time with my son. I was hoping for a week-on-week-off schedule. My heart and mind were vested in the endeavor to support my son and have equal parenting time. I had never asked for more than half the parenting time with my son, since Noni and I were equally his parents. Before I filed the motion with the court, I needed to build a case and find a new attorney. My first thought was to meet with the psychologist and ask if he would testify in court, since my son had shared his feelings with him many times. The psychologist agreed to testify for my son's sake.

The next step was to find a reputable attorney in family law that had a good track record. When I had previously met with the psychologist he referred me to a parents' rights activist in town who had been through something similar to my situation. We met at his house for an hour and discussed my situation. He also shared his past experiences with me regarding his fight for parental equality. He had already lost custody, but through a court modification in parenting time, he had gone from having his child 9 percent of the time to 50 percent. He shared his attorney's name with me, and I contacted her after our meeting to schedule an appointment.

The attorney lived two hours north of town, but I did not care. I just wanted positive results. My only reservation was that the attorney would not have a rapport with the local judges, and she would not be familiar with the opposing attorney to know what we were going up against. In our initial meeting, I learned that the attorney had adopted many sons. To me, this meant that she had a compassionate heart. It also felt like she was in family law for the right reason: to help children. I liked the way the meeting started. When the attorney and I discussed my son, she expressed her concerns about his young age.

Since he was six years old at the time, he would not be able to testify. In the state of Oregon there is no specific age for when a child can testify, but having my son speak to the court would not be considered appropriate. I had to be his voice. At the end of the meeting, I hired the attorney.

She told me to go home and get all my documentation together while she filed the motion with the court to modify parenting time. I returned home and spent several days compiling documentation I had gathered through the years. Once I had the documentation organized in a bullet point format, I sent it off to the attorney. She did not like the organization of the Microsoft Word document I sent, so she had her assistant transfer the information to an Excel format. The modification in parenting time was filed with the court, and the court date was set. The opposing party requested from the court that I be responsible for Noni's attorney fees because I was the petitioner, and my request was allegedly unwarranted.

In preparing for trial, my attorney said that our strategy was basic and simple. Our position was that I was a good father, and Noni was a good mother. My attorney's proposed strategy was difficult for me to accept. There was so much dysfunction to share with the court, and I had already prepared the documentation. I felt like the truth needed to be said about Noni's destructive behavior and her inability to put my son first. When I contested my attorney's strategy, she insisted that it would work. While we took the high road in court, the opposing party would attack. Then the judge would see where the problems lay, and Noni would seal her own fate. The phrase the attorney used to explain the strategy was, "Don't look a gift horse in the mouth!" It meant that we should not challenge the onslaught of attacks but be grateful for them.

The opposing party also planned their strategy. It was the Karl Rove strategy, to zealously attack my strengths and turn them into weaknesses. Their goal was to discredit my desire and ability to be a half-time father.

The trial date arrived, and I was so nervous that I could not eat. It was ironic that I was fearful of court, yet I was the one who petitioned for the trial. I arrived at the courthouse and found my attorney in the lobby. It was apparent she was not feeling well because of a terrible cold that had just hit her. She said that she considered postponing trial, but she did not want me to have to wait any longer to potentially secure more time with my son. Then, we walked down the hall together to get our assigned judge and courtroom. On the way, we encountered Noni and her attorney and made introductions. It was cordial.

Both attorneys were wearing women's business suits. I was wearing slacks, a button-down dress shirt, and a New York Cosmos soccer jacket. Noni was wearing drab khakis with an earth-tone cotton shirt. Her hair was wet, and she was not wearing any makeup. It was obvious the attorneys had selected our wardrobes to reflect the characters we would develop. I was going to be the active soccer dad, and she was going to be the oppressed martyr mom.

After our introduction, we all walked over to the chambers where we received our assigned judge and courtroom number. When the facilitator read our assignment, she inquired how long the trial needed to be. My attorney suggested a half-day trial, but the opposing attorney stuck two fingers in the air and demanded a two-day trial. There was persuasion in her voice and conviction in her body language. I instantly regretted my decision to pursue more parenting time though court. After getting the assigned courtroom number, we walked back down the hallway to it. Noni also walked with her attorney along the opposite side of the hallway and looked fearful. They were both already in character. We filed into the courtroom and took our places.

The judge that was assigned to our case was a retired judge from a conservative county in Southern Oregon. He was filling in that day, as part of his Public Employee Retirement System (PERS) obligation through the State of Oregon Judge Member Program. Before the court proceedings commenced, I tried to forewarn my attorney that we were in the calm before the storm. Since she was under the weather, her primary concerns were her runny nose, sore throat, and the next lozenge. The judge entered the courtroom, and we all stood in his honor. He was introduced to the courtroom, and we all took our seats again. My attorney's opening comments were about how I was a good father and how badly my son wanted more parenting time with me. It was very basic and simple. The opposing party set their tone by accusing me of badgering Noni, rather than advocating for my son. From there, they focused on discrediting me as a father and a human being.

To imply I was dishonest, the opposition claimed that I bribed my son to request having more time in my care. They claimed I had promised him a guinea pig if we got more time together. The ironic reality was that my son and I already had a guinea pig, and her name was Loretta. Loretta had three babies, and we gave one of the babies to Noni. She kept it for a little while but then sold the rodent online.

To demonstrate I was malicious, they claimed that I had purposely scheduled my son's soccer team practices on Noni's parenting days. The truth of the matter was that she had him every day of the school week except Thursdays and every other Friday.

To suggest I was aggressive, they claimed I had gotten a red card in an adult league soccer match and had been kicked off my soccer team. The fact was that I had never received a red card in my life nor been kicked off a soccer team. And most importantly, this claim had nothing to do with parenting.

To display I had poor parental guidance, they explained that I let our son watch King of the Hill. The truth was that we *had* watched King of the Hill, and we liked it. My son was six years old, and the cartoon is relatively benign.

To reveal I had a drug problem, they claimed that I smoked marijuana and that they had my paraphernalia. This was coming from a habitual marijuana user who grew marijuana and who smoked it throughout her pregnancy and for the duration of her breastfeeding.

To convey I was abusive, they alleged that I had hit my son at his grandmother's eightieth birthday party. The accurate scenario was that my son had tried to run outside during the celebration, and I had tried to stop him, and he fell. We were at a community park, and there was nobody outside to watch him. Besides, he needed to be there for the family celebration.

To propose I was negligent, they accused me of leaving my son with my close friend and his wife, who had just moved here from her native country of Korea. Noni accused the woman of touching my son's genitals. Due to the allegations, my son has never been around the woman again, and my relationship with my lifelong friend has been strained.

To submit I was disrespectful, they claimed that I called Noni nasty names. The irony was that I remembered, regretfully, having called her one derogatory name that was not in her arsenal. It was *psycho*, and it was too close to home for her to divulge.

When it was my attorney's turn to cross-examine Noni, she did not address Noni's unstable behaviors nor her fabricated accusations. She stuck to the plan: I was a good father and my opponent was a good mother. Instead of digging our feet into the sand, we went high while they went low. I asked my attorney why she did not refute the false allegations that were made about me to set the record straight with the judge. She had all my documentation at her fingertips, and I was frantically writing her notes during my opponent's examination, explaining what was untrue. Her response to me was, "Don't look a gift horse in the mouth!" The judge would see where the problem was. I understood the strategy, but I was skeptical that it would work.

The opposing party had four character witnesses who took the stand. They were the custody evaluator, a teacher from the old preschool, a mother from the old preschool, and a mother from our birthing class more than six years prior. It was difficult for me to see the faces of the people that were in favor of keeping my son from me. The custody evaluator testified that our parental relationship was high-conflict. He also said that my son needed a primary residence, which was already at Noni's house.

A teacher from the old preschool testified that Noni and I could not get along. She was my son's homeroom teacher at the time I stopped accepting breast milk ice cubes that Noni would leave for me in the classroom freezer.

A mother from the old preschool testified that she saw me pointing at Noni in the hallway, four years prior, when my son was a toddler. I had just moved out of my house, and Noni would not allow me to have him. She'd spent a lot of her time at the preschool guarding him from me, like I was an animal wanting to eat its young. I remember the moment I had pointed at her. It was to tell her that she was violating my parental rights and that she did not own my son.

A mother from the birthing class testified that I had confronted her at a soccer event, after we had dropped our children off, to ask why she had been a character witness in my prior custody evaluation. I had thought it was a fair question to ask. She used to be my next-door neighbor, and I thought we had good rapport. I also thought she may be able to explain something I was unaware of. Instead, the woman started yelling at me, and I said to her, "Just forget it!" However, in the courtroom she changed my words to "Fuck you!" The words were lost in translation. After the fact, I thought back to when we were neighbors, and I had helped her husband (per his request) move out of their house to be with another woman.

My attorney thought fewer character witnesses were better. We had three character witnesses: my son's psychologist, the best friend I lived with through the separation, and the teacher who defended my right to visit my son at his preschool. The psychologist testified that my son felt strongly about spending more time in my care and that his request was consistent. After he testified, he walked over to Noni, shook her hand, and said that he hoped his testimony would not negatively impact her. Then he came over to me, shook my hand, and said the very same thing. My best friend testified that he trusted me with his own children and that I was a devoted and loving father. Then he said, "To suggest otherwise, would be ludicrous!" My son's preschool teacher testified over the speaker phone in the courtroom, which was all she was willing to do. When she was asked questions, she repeated herself that both parents were equally involved at the preschool while my son had attended there.

In the closing arguments, the opposing attorney looked at me with contempt. She summarized all her client's claims in a convincing monolog. I was not the father who was advocating for my child, parental equality, and family balance. I was the ogre ex-husband that was badgering her client. My attorney followed with her closing arguments. She emphasized that I was a good father and that my son desired more time with me. Then she drew a giant cup on a white board with a horizontal line through the middle. It was a visual aid that symbolized parenthood. The line through the middle represented two equal halves. Since we were equally his parents, we deserved equal parenting time to make the cup full for our child.

After the judge listened to the closing arguments, he was ready to give his verdict. I was skeptical of my chances once again, and the pending verdict felt like a forgone conclusion. Everything that could have gone wrong seemed to have gone wrong. The opposing attorney had attacked me for two days, and I had no defense. My attorney would have rather been home in bed, and the retired judge seemed disinterested in my request. Just as I presumed, the judge was unsupportive of my cause. His ruling was that the parenting time would remain the same and that I was responsible for Noni's attorney fees. In his closing comments, the judge looked over at me and gave me some inaccurate and unsolicited advice. He told me to make the best of the time that I had with my son and to turn off the damn TV! I could not have been more misjudged or humiliated.

My attorney objected to the ruling, but the judge overruled her objection. He said that I could write him a letter to contest his decision and then slammed down his gavel. My world was spinning because I had not considered this outcome. I could have handled the verdict of status quo, but having to pay the opposing attorney—who insisted on the two-day production—was crippling. As my attorney and I exited the courtroom, Noni and her attorney were embracing in celebration. I could not understand how she fought so hard against me and my son's desire to spend more time together. It was more important for her to go into battle and win the war.

Once we arrived outside, I asked my attorney why she had not defended me. Her response was that she had thought her strategy would work. She added that she would do it all over again in the same fashion. She was unwilling to admit her poor preparation and poor representation. I followed up by asking her why she thought her strategy had not worked. Her reply was that she had misread the judge and he was just not interested. I felt certain that my attorney had never read my documentation or studied my case.

I was stunned and desperate and asked my attorney if there was another way I could appeal the ruling besides writing a letter to the judge. She mentioned the appellate court but highly suggested against it. She told me to write the letter to the judge, and said she would reach out to the opposing attorney to discuss a partial forgiveness in debt. After speaking with my attorney outside the courthouse, I had to drive straight to soccer practice to coach my son. Noni was already there, sharing her victory and getting hugs from other mothers, while I coached their kids.

The following day, I wrote my letter to the judge. It stated that I had taken the high road in court and that I had been there to advocate for my son. I also asked him to reconsider requiring me to pay Noni's attorney fees. A few weeks later, I received a letter with his denial to my request. My attorney also contacted the opposing attorney to ask if she would accept less than the full fee amount—we still did not know how much it was going to be. Because the opposing attorney did not represent me, she could have charged me any amount within reason, and I would have no idea if it was accurate. It was on the honor system, so I knew I was hosed. In the end, the opposing attorney was unwilling to offer me any monetary relief. I was out of options.

My price of admission for the two-day trial was $40,000. I was beside myself and had no idea how I was going to come up with the funds. Aside from court, I had also just gone into debt another $7,000 for lifesaving surgery on my new female golden retriever. She had been hit by a speeding truck in front of my house and both of her lungs had been punctured. My best friend had joked at the time that it was the best money I had ever spent. He'd said my dog would pull me out of a well someday and save my life.

I was a middle-class single father who had committed financial suicide. After meeting with my sister, who understands federal tax codes, I cashed out the principal balance of my Roth IRA and my son's college fund. Ironically, the funds I had stock piled for my son's future were also the funds used to pay Noni's attorney. In full disclosure, the funds I had liquidated were still not enough to cover my debt. I held my attorney professionally responsible for laying an egg, and she decreased my balance by $8,000. To pay off my dog's surgery, I applied for Care Credit, and I am still paying it off.

The financial loss I suffered was like losing a loved

one. I did not realize how important money was to me until I was deep in the hole. My depression was at an all-time low, and I felt like I was stuck in a bad dream. I could not eat, sleep, or stop obsessing. I dropped twenty pounds in twenty days, and my professional work was suffering. I had to dig deep and get it together before I lost everything.

I visited my physician, who offered me pharmaceutical assistance. For the short term, he prescribed Valium to relax me and to decrease my anxiety. I also experimented with acupuncture therapy and found it very helpful. I thought the pins in my body would feel uncomfortable, but at each visit I fell into a slumber and woke rejuvenated. Exercise was more critical than usual, and I found a daily yoga class that helped my mind, body, and spirit. I also visited the couples' counselor again to seek more of his wisdom. In our session, we discussed my monetary losses. He reminded me that no matter what happened to me financially, I would always have a roof over my head. If I completely lost everything, a loved one would take me in. That was more than many people had, and I needed to feel thankful for what mattered the most: my health, family, and friends. I was crying with a full belly again, and I needed to get back to the basics of life.

CHAPTER FIFTEEN

# The Gap

The saying goes, "At least you still have your health," and it was an optimistic reminder that my glass was half full. As I focused on my health and mindset, I entrenched myself in state family law. I wanted to better understand how the law was broken and how it could be improved to make a positive difference for parents and their children in the future. Somehow, I wanted to turn my metaphoric pile of lemons into delicious lemonade.

I started my research by visiting my son's psychologist since he had seen it all from the standpoint of humanity. He felt strongly that the zero-sum game of sole custody was a travesty and that the court could do a much better job to preserve the best interests and welfare of children through parental involvement and family balance. It wasn't about job security for attorneys or simple choices for judges; it was about the real world and real life!

The psychologist had witnessed the darkest side of humanity due to custody disputes. He worked with the victims of the zero-sum game: the children. In some cases, they were the surviving children. He taught me the word *filicide*, which means the deliberate act of a parent killing his or her own child. In many cases, sole custody disputes were the catalyst for noncustodial parents turning to the dark side and snapping on their children. He recognized the correlation between the two and witnessed how sole custody disputes could bring the Hyde out of Jekyll. Everyone has a dark side and a custody battle can be its trigger!

The psychologist and I discussed potential solutions to the conundrum of sole custody. He firmly believed that the court should default to the presumption of joint custody unless there was substantial evidence to suggest otherwise. His decades of experience in working with children taught him this. A disagreement between two parents did not warrant sole custody. A disagreement between two parents warranted a parenting coordinator that could assist them in finding resolution.

Another flaw in state family law that we discussed was that judges were required to reach a permanent decision in sole custody disputes with very little—often distorted—information. Their decision also needed to be made in the span of a trial. The snapshot format did not allow judges to really understand the situation. In disputed cases, there needed to be a cooling period before any permanent decisions were made regarding the best interests and welfare of a child.

The psychologist suggested to me that a mandatory one-year cooling period should be required before any permanent decisions were made by the court. It would comprise shared parenting time and decision making. If the parents could not agree on a temporary arrangement, they could appoint or hire a parenting coordinator to assist them. In many cases, the parenting coordinator could determine an acceptable solution for the parents before the cooling period has expired. But if not, the parenting coordinator could give his or her recommendation to the court. After the cooling period, the coordinator would have a good understanding of the best interests and welfare of the child.

A parenting coordinator could also act as a monitor for children as they mature to adulthood. Currently, the permanent decision of sole custody can be a sentence for a child. To have a voice for change, the child may have to take legal action against his or her own parent in court. A parenting coordinator would offer the opportunity for a child to have a legal voice. The parenting coordinator could also help parenting plans evolve along with the child's best interests and welfare as the child grew to adulthood.

My next visit was with the parents' rights activist who I had met with before. He also attested to the detriments of sole custody and understood how it stripped a child of natural parental involvement and family balance. We met several times for lunch, collaborated on understanding the negative effects of sole custody, and identified where state family law was broken.

There are two contradictory statutes, one of which is the reason for the zero-sum-game of sole custody.

Oregon Revised Statute 107.169(3) states, "The court shall not order joint custody unless both parents agree to the terms and conditions of the order," while ORS 107.137(1) claims, "In determining custody of a minor child, the court shall give primary consideration to the best interests and welfare of the child." A judge cannot rule joint custody unless both parents agree, but sole custody is not in the best interests and welfare of the child. It is presumptuous of the court to expect parents to agree on anything during the peak of their dissolution. But to place the child in the middle of the conflict, as an award, is inflammatory to the process and counterproductive to preserving the family dynamic.

One could argue that ORS 107.169(3) violates the Fourteenth Amendment to the United States Constitution, "…nor shall any state deprive any person of life, liberty, or property, without due process of law.…" A parent can have his or her life liberty to make major decisions in the best interests and welfare of the child taken away, simply because the other parent did not agree with joint custody. Is that due process? The only benefits of ORS 107.169(3) go to family-law attorneys and judges. The attorneys get a steady income stream fed by the conflict, and judges get an easy decision: heads or tails.

I remember thinking to myself, "The solution is simple!" The state could just remove three words from ORS 107.169(3) and replace them with five words. Instead of reading, "The court *shall not* order joint custody, *unless* both parents agree to the terms and conditions of the order," the statute could read, "The court *may* order joint custody, *even if* both parents *do not* agree to the terms and conditions of the order." This would allow the court to give primary consideration to the best interests and welfare of the child, regardless of the parents' petitions.

Another alternative the activist and I discussed is for the court to divide up the major decisions of custody, just as it does with parenting time. If mother is a doctor and father is an educator, it would be appropriate for mother to make decisions regarding healthcare and father to make decisions regarding education. This solution would eliminate the zero-sum game of sole custody and preserve the family balance.

With this alternative, the court would lose no authority and so much would be gained. The court could still assign all the major decisions of custody to one parent, if necessary. But it could also custom tailor parenting arrangements to more accurately correspond to a child's best interests and welfare. This would better support the claim of ORS 107.137(1) that the court will give primary consideration to the best interests and welfare of the child.

After researching the contradictions in state family law, the activist and I studied past bills that had been written for prior legislative sessions. The bills usually involved the recommendation of the presumption of joint custody, and they all died in committee. They either didn't get passed, or they were never voted on. We also studied the most recent state research done by a parental involvement workgroup that was formed by the Oregon State Family Law Advisory Committee (SFLAC) in 2010. It was a multidisciplinary workgroup that was established to review developmental research, family court patterns, and legislative policies.

The workgroup claimed to have investigated local and national trends regarding best-interests standards and practices for children of divorce. This investigation was the basis of their research. But when I looked at their sources, many of them were research studies completed in Australia, which has a different history, different laws, and a different culture. This was my first warning that the workgroup had been a failure. In the workgroup's summary report dated March, 2011, their findings contradict their own research. The workgroup recognized that angry, uncooperative, and litigious parents were disruptive to a child's sense of security and stability. They also acknowledged that custody and parenting-time decisions impacted children and families for the rest of their lives. However, the final recommendation of the workgroup was that, in high-conflict custody disputes, sole custody and weighted parenting time are the best solutions.

The contradictions in state family law and the findings of the SFLAC parental involvement workgroup research were similar. They both claimed to have the child's best interests standards as their foundation, but ORS 107.169(3) handcuffed the court to fulfill their claims. The reality is, that both the state and workgroup had it backwards. They believed that high-conflict disputes were a reason for sole custody, instead of the weapon of sole custody being a reason for high-conflict disputes. It was a chicken-before-the-egg scenario.

Oregon Revised Statute 107.169(3) is the culprit in the high-conflict disagreements and disputes. It is the vehicle for war and the child goes to the winner. If disagreeable parents knew the court had the ability to rule joint custody, regardless of their antics or desires, that knowledge would change the roadmap of litigation. It would be less about discrediting the other parent and more about seeking an amenable solution in the best interests and welfare of their child.

The workgroup claimed that the state of Oregon avoids one-size-fits-all presumptions (i.e., joint custody) and encourages custom-tailored arrangements that accurately correspond with a child's best interests. But, ORS 107.169(3) doesn't allow that. In cases where one parent refuses to agree on joint custody, the outcome is black and white.

If the court could select which parent is most appropriate for each of the major decision-making responsibilities of custody, it could, in actuality, custom-tailor parenting arrangements that correspond accurately with a child's best interests. This process would also promote productive negotiations between the parents (and their attorneys). If parents cannot agree to share the major decisions regarding their child, they could divide them up, instead of drawing a line in the sand. This format would also ensure the involvement of both parents in the child's life and preserve the family balance.

The workgroup was hypocritical in their findings, and the state is as well in their claim to consider the best interests and welfare of our children. Oregon Revised Statute 107.169(3) promotes litigation and supports the special interests of attorneys. After all, it is attorneys who create such laws, and it seems that their interests come before those of our children.

CHAPTER SIXTEEN

# The Squeaky Wheel

After interviewing the psychologist, collaborating with the parents' rights activist, and researching state family law, I understood where the law was broken and thought of ways to fix it. I thought it was simple, and I had all the answers. The next step was to get the information into the hands of the politicians who create our laws. I had never lobbied for anything before, but I had never felt so passionate about anything like this. In May, 2012, I started my campaign by writing a summary email to a constituent state senator and member of the Oregon House of Representatives explaining the broken law:

> Subject: Oregon Family Law – Child Custody
>
> Dear Senator & Member of the House:
>
> Currently, it is not possible in the state of Oregon for the court to rule joint custody if both parents are not in agreement. This is a contradiction in the state law and breaches my civil liberties as a parent.

Although ORS 107.137(1) states, "The court shall give primary consideration to the best interests and welfare of the child," the court must rule sole custody. This poses the question: how can the court give primary consideration to the best interests and welfare of the child when the court is limited to rule sole custody in all cases where the parents cannot agree to joint custody?

In my research, I have interviewed professionals in our community within the fields of child psychology and child welfare. In all cases, these professionals have agreed across the board that a high percentage of custody cases should result in joint custody. This is the most beneficial option for our children and their parents. In many cases, separation is adversarial, and to give one parent the authority to make all major life decisions regarding the child skews the balance of parenting. If both parents are able and willing to be actively involved in their child's life, they should both be able to participate in major life decisions regarding their child. This offers the best balance for the child's best interests and welfare.

Sole custody is appropriate in cases where one parent is abusive, dangerous, psychologically or mentally challenged, addicted to drugs, or absent from the child's life. The result of sole legal custody is to legally disenfranchise one parent from the child. It strips them of their civil liberty to participate in major life decisions regarding their child. It is unjust that the state of Oregon must rule sole custody just because one parent will simply not agree to joint custody.

It is only fair for the court to have the ability to rule joint custody regardless of the parents' wishes. We have progressed in many ways as a society, culture, and nation where women are equal in the workforce and can go into combat in war. Let's not continue to hold fathers—who are the noncustodial parent five out of six times—back from being equal parents. Moreover, let's stop handcuffing our judges and give them the tools necessary to truly give primary consideration to the best interests and welfare of our children.

The US Census Bureau (2009) reports that "about 1 in 6 custodial parents are fathers." However, ORS 107.137(1) claims, "no preference in custody shall be given to the mother over the father for the sole reason that she is the mother...."

A holistic solution for situations where parents cannot agree on life decisions regarding their children is to offer them a parenting coordinator. This can be a self-subsidized, fee-based service offered by the state, or the parties could mutually agree on appointing their own parenting coordinator. This is a more productive alternative than hiring private attorneys who are adversarial by their job description. Thank you for your time and consideration.

Best regards,

Joseph Cowles

After sending the emails to the senator and member of the House, I followed up with phone calls. I wanted to make sure they read what I sent them, and I wanted to request a follow-up meeting in person. To my delight, they both had read the emails and granted me a face-to-face meeting at the capitol building in Salem.

Our meeting was scheduled for thirty minutes and we discussed the contents of my email. At the end of the meeting, the senator recommended I contact the chair of the Oregon State Judiciary Committee, who was also a constituent senator from my town. I reached out to him by telephone, and he agreed to meet with me at a local coffee shop downtown.

For this meeting, I put together a presentation. My goal was to share a new idea: give the court the power to assign each of the major decision-making responsibilities in custody disputes, just as they assign parenting time. This would give the court the ability to custom-tailor parenting arrangements that accurately correspond to the best interests and welfare of a child.

I showed up to the coffee shop a few minutes early and stood on the sidewalk in my power suit and tie with my briefcase. The chairman, wearing a flannel button-down shirt and jeans, showed up a few minutes later on his commuter bicycle. After parking his bicycle, he pulled a comb out of his back pocket and groomed his grey hair. I recognized him from his photo and walked over to introduce myself. My first impression was that the chairman was very approachable and incredibly down to earth. After our introductions, we walked into the coffee shop and sat at an empty table. I offered to buy him coffee but he politely declined. Without hesitation, I started my presentation.

My introduction addressed the core of the problem in state family law. I cited ORS 107.169(3), "The court shall not order joint custody, unless both parents agree to the terms and conditions of the order." This is a Hobson's Choice and does not grant judges the power to rule in the best interests and welfare of the child. I also mentioned that prior bills had attempted to implement the *presumption* of joint custody, but it seemed to be too strong of a shift from the current paradigm of family law.

Before I could reveal the unprecedented hybrid solution of dividing up custodial responsibilities, the chairman interjected and exclaimed, "Been there, done that!" He explained that the issue of legal custody was too charged with strong feelings on both sides of the issue. For this reason, past bills regarding custody had died in committee. To me, his mindset was counterintuitive. If the topic was so polarizing, it deserved the most attention. It needed to be discussed to find resolution.

The chairman followed up with another barrier. He told me to think of law as a string puppet and the statutes as the strings. Any movement in one statute created flexion or tension in other statutes. I understood his analogy and appreciated his candor. I also felt his resistance.

The perspectives of the chairman were a perfect segue for the next topic in my presentation. I had an unprecedented, logical solution that would allow the court to do what the state says it is should do: give primary consideration to the best interests and welfare of the child. We needed to focus on doing what is right for our children, not on the workload required to do so.

My solution was to empower judges with the ability to assign custodial responsibilities, just as they could assign parenting time. The current law legally disenfranchises one parent from their child (with sole custody), increases the division between the parents, and threatens the family balance. It also increases the percentage of uninvolved parents who have lost their custodial rights. My solution would benefit the court, giving it more power; the parents, who could stay involved; and the children, who would no longer be the award of a sole custody dispute. It would be a vast improvement over the zero-sum game of sole custody, which continues to rip families apart.

The chairman of the Judiciary Committee was the figurehead I needed to influence. If I could get him to acknowledge that the current law was broken and that I had an unprecedented, yet basic, solution for the committee, Senate, and House, I might get traction. He was the mainline to progress! I followed my claim with a valid example: If mother is a pediatrician and dad is a tenured educator, it is reasonable to assume that mother should make decisions regarding healthcare and father should make decisions regarding education. The current law does not allow the court to reach this decision, due to ORS 107.169(3). After multiple meetings at the same coffee shop, the chairman granted me an informational hearing with the Judiciary Committee.

After I was granted the hearing, I asked the psychologist to join me in my presentation. He had his own professional reasons why he wanted to fight for our common goal. He explained to me that between birth and age five a female child is approximately ten times more likely to die from parental abuse, neglect, or filicide than an adult woman is likely to die from domestic violence at any time of her adult life. He identified custody disputes as a major contributing factor to this horrifying statistic.

The child psychologist agreed to join me for the informational hearing. Since he had a PhD in psychology and had worked with extreme child custody cases, I felt he could add professional insight and impact to the hearing. I then put together another presentation using an effective format I had learned in graduate school: 1. Tell the audience what you are about to tell them. 2. Tell them. 3. Tell the audience what you just told them. My repetitive message would leave no room for error.

The day came to present to the Judiciary Committee. The chairman asked the psychologist and me to state our names for the committee, and we had the floor. I started with an overview of the topics I would be covering in the hearing. My claim was that current state family law was conflicted, and legal custody disputes left judges with an all-or-nothing scenario. The law didn't give judges the power to rule in the best interests and welfare of our children.

I followed my claim of broken law with a discussion of the adverse effects of sole custody. It was a legal sentence for some children who never had a voice or a choice. It was a permanent decision, and there were no legal third-party monitors in place through which a child could be heard. There were only attorneys and litigation. Mediation did not work for disagreeable parents, and, in these cases, judges needed the appropriate arrows in their quivers. The power to assign each of the custodial responsibilities to the most appropriate parent would enhance the court's arsenal. Judges could custom-tailor custodial responsibilities, just as they did parenting time.

The psychologist had been silent up to this point but then took the floor at the perfect moment. He expressed his concern that legal custody disputes and sole custody killed children. It was a valid view from a doctor in psychology who worked with these types of cases. The psychologist also discussed the difficulties parents experience when trying to agree on joint custody during the peak of their dissolution. There needed to be a mandatory cooling period for high-conflict cases, and parenting coordinators ought to be assigned for cases that needed them. The coordinators could either be appointed by the court or privately hired. They could also act as a sounding board for children as they grew into adulthood.

From my perspective, the solution was in our grasp. With our solution, neither parent needed to be legally disenfranchised from their child. The mandatory cooling period would diffuse most custody disputes, and in cases that don't get resolved, parenting coordinators could help find resolution. If the parents and coordinator were unsuccessful at finding resolution, the coordinator could give a recommendation to the court at the end of the cooling period. The recommendation would be based on the documentation of the cooling period, instead of a distorted snapshot of reality in court.

The parenting coordinator could recommend the court to split up the custodial responsibilities or to assign them all to one parent (when needed) and the court could custom-tailor parenting arrangements on a case-by-case basis and move away from the hard line of sole custody. Judges would have the option to accept the recommendation of the parenting coordinator or tweak the recommendation to their satisfaction. They would finally have the power to "give primary consideration to the best interests and welfare of our children!"

In closing, I highlighted everything I had already covered and reminded the committee that we could do much better for our children! Then I asked how we could move forward to make a difference for the children and parents of the future. Oregon Revised Statute 107.169(3) had already ripped too many families apart, and it was time to stop the bleeding.

Our campaign to preserve parenthood and to protect the family balance was heard. The chairman of the committee recommended we form a new state-appointed workgroup to find a better solution than the current zero-sum game of sole custody. He explained that the workgroup would be diverse, and it would consist of collaborators from multiple professional sectors, not just law and politics. The chairman exclaimed, "This time, I want to do it right!"

The hearing ended, and the campaign had escalated. The squeaky wheel warranted the grease.

CHAPTER SEVENTEEN
# The Workgroup

The workgroup was assembled by the Judiciary Committee and our coordinator scheduled the first meeting. It was at the state capitol building, where all our meetings were to be held. The first meeting date arrived and I drove up to Salem to meet the workgroup. I arrived a few minutes early and took a seat in the lobby to cram my notes. About ten minutes later, while I was studying, the psychologist arrived in the lobby. We said hello and did a quick overview of the meeting as we searched for the conference room. Although our reasons for participating in the workgroup were very different, we shared the same mission: to advocate for children's rights, parental equality, and family balance.

We found the conference room and took our seats. Other members of the workgroup, who all knew each other, trickled into the room individually. It was an intimate setting of only seven workgroup members:

- the Judiciary Committee counsel and administrator (workgroup coordinator)

- the public affairs director—Oregon State Bar
- the legislative advocacy director—Oregon Law Center
- the manager of the family-law program—Oregon Judicial Department
- a family-law attorney from Salem
- the psychologist
- the end-user (me).

I was surprised by the Judiciary Committee's selections for the workgroup. The chairman had mentioned that it would be a diverse group with various backgrounds. I had taken his words out of context and was expecting more representation from human services. The psychologist and I were the only two members who didn't have a background in law. And besides the family-law attorney from Salem, we were the only men. We were the minority in more ways than one, but we needed to have influence for our cause. Our work was cut out for us!

After introductions, the coordinator asked me to speak about my situation and firsthand experiences within state family law. I summarized my difficult separation experience and discussed the uphill battle to be involved in my son's life. It was the initial reason I pursued legal action. I had experienced attorneys, mediation, a custody evaluation, and litigation. And they were all similar experiences in that they had consistent outcomes. I was kept from my son, and I failed him. That was why I was sitting in that room: I had tried everything else and failed. My experiences were what led me to lobbying, because I had nothing left. I had less time with my son, no custodial authority, and I committed financial suicide trying to advocate for him. There were better solutions, and I was optimistic about exploring them with the workgroup!

The second workgroup meeting was scheduled about a month later. I arrived early, but this time I didn't see the psychologist in the lobby beforehand. He arrived at the conference room just as the meeting started, and he immediately demanded the floor. His message was that his role in the workgroup was not to be confused with my case. He had a professional interest for improving state family law, and it did not have to do with my personal situation. It had to do with filicide that resulted from volatile legal custody disputes. The room stayed silent, and the psychologist paused. He reached down to his shoulder bag lying on the floor by his chair and pulled something out of it. It was a blown-up picture of two young children. He passed it around the room. After everyone had a look at the picture, the psychologist pointed at one of the children and said, "I work with this child." Then he pointed at the other and said, "I would like to work with this child too but I can't, because he is dead!" The children in the picture were the children of Amanda Jo Stott-Smith. She had thrown these children off the Sellwood Bridge and into the Willamette river in Portland, Oregon, and only one of them survived. When the police had questioned Stott-Smith about her horrific act of filicide, she confessed that she had attempted to kill her own children to get revenge on her estranged husband, who had just obtained sole custody a month prior.

The members of the workgroup were irritated by the psychologist's powerful presentation and his visual aid. We were there to discuss family law, they said, and he was being disruptive to the meeting. One member complained about his antics and claimed that he was pulling the workgroup off track. The workgroup collectively dismissed the psychologist's example of the extreme consequences of sole custody disputes, but the psychologist held his ground. He shared with the group what he had already shared with me: a female child, from birth to age five, is approximately ten times more likely to die from parental abuse, neglect, or filicide than any adult woman is likely to die from domestic violence at any time of her adult life. This was the national average, but the state of Oregon (with its preference for sole custody) had a filicide rate that was 2.5 times the national average.

Instead of absorbing the link between filicide and legal custody disputes, some of the workgroup members seemed offended by the psychologist's example and statistics. The example he had used was of a mother who was the murderer, and the statistic he had shared was that little girls were ten times more likely to die from parental abuse than grown women were to die from domestic abuse.

After the second meeting, I caught up with the psychologist outside and asked him why he went on his crusade. He explained that he was protecting himself from Noni's attorney. She had called him directly following the first workgroup meeting and attempted to intimidate him out of continuing his participation in the workgroup, claiming conflict of interest regarding his association with my son. He had to make it clear to the workgroup, which contained a mole, that he was not participating due to my situation. He had his own reasons, which he fully disclosed. I was shocked to hear what the psychologist told me, but it made sense why he had been so passionate during his unexpected workgroup monologue. It also explained why Noni had found another psychologist for my son.

When I asked the psychologist who the informant was, he said that he suspected it was the workgroup member who was a family-law attorney in Salem. I had to find out if this was the case. Plus, there was something else I wanted to ask the attorney from Salem.

The suspected attorney was approachable, and I emailed him with an invitation to have coffee with me. He accepted my offer, and we met at a coffee shop near the capitol building. There were two discussion points on my agenda. The first was that I was worried about my son's struggles at his mother's house, and I wanted to help him get more time with me. This desire of his was consistent, and I wanted to know if there was any avenue that I had not thought of for my son to have a legal voice. The second topic of discussion was whether he had contacted Noni's attorney to notify her that the psychologist and I were involved in the workgroup.

When the attorney and I met, I started with the first subject. How could I help my son have his own voice with the court? The attorney told me there existed a statute in state family law that would allow my son to have a voice. Oregon Revised Statute 107.425(6) states:

> The court, on its own motion or on the motion of a party, may appoint counsel for the children. However, if requested to do so by one or more of the children, the court shall appoint counsel for the child or children. A reasonable fee for an attorney so appointed may be charged against one or more of the parties or as a cost in the proceedings but shall not be charged against funds appropriated for public defense services.

My son could write a letter to the presiding judge of my county, and the court would have to appoint him an attorney; he could finally have his own voice. However, I needed to table the prospective solution, as I wasn't sure that it would be a healthy environment or experience for a ten-year-old boy.

I moved to the second discussion item on my agenda. I asked the attorney if he had contacted Noni's attorney after the first workgroup meeting to inform her that the psychologist and I were part of the workgroup. He hesitated to respond and then waffled around the question. He said that he knew who the attorney was, but he did not admit to contacting her. So, I asked him again bluntly if he was the person who contacted her and he admitted to being her informant.

By the third workgroup meeting, we started to discuss prospective solutions to the problems of current family law that we identified in the first two meetings. I mentioned the unprecedented solution of the court being able to assign custodial responsibilities between two parents if they could not co-parent. It would give judges more power to rule in the best interests and welfare of children. However, the consensus of the workgroup was that judges did not want a choice. They claimed my solution would only increase conflict in cases where the parents could not agree to co-parent. They believed that one parent needed to have all the custodial responsibilities to eliminate conflict, and it seemed to be the mother. Then the attorney from Salem nonchalantly said that if he ever got a divorce, his wife would definitely get custody. It was as if legal custody was trivial. He appeared to be numb to the process and to the significance sole custody would have in his and his children's lives.

I disagreed with the workgroup's opinion, and so did the psychologist. He expressed that joint custody should be the presumption and that it should take more than a purposeful disagreement for a parent to win or lose custody. If a parent loses custody of his or her child, it should be for more significant reasons. Legal custody disputes rip families apart and that is an abomination of our legal system. Legally disenfranchising a parent from his or her child is not the answer to custody disputes. According to the psychologist, in almost all cases, joint custody is in the best interests and welfare of a child, regardless of the parents' desires.

The workgroup environment was heated, and the psychologist continued to shake things up. He looked across the table at the attorney from Salem and claimed that he was hurting children when he left his morals outside the courtroom door to litigate custody disputes. The attorney defended himself and declared that he never checked his morals at the door. He would fire his client before he would consider doing anything immoral. The workgroup was divided, once again. The psychologist was the obvious wild card, and rightfully so. His profession was working with broken families and scarred children, and legal custody disputes were a major contributing factor to their condition. He wasn't an attorney looking for his next revenue-generating custody dispute. He was a doctor in psychology who wanted to help children. After the verbal dispute between the psychologist and attorney, the workgroup coordinator made an executive decision. She looked over at me and the psychologist and insisted that she would disband the workgroup if we continued to push for a presumption of joint custody.

After the third workgroup session, the psychologist and I spoke outside of the capitol building to reconvene. We discussed how the workgroup coordinator, who also worked as counsel for the Judiciary Committee, stonewalled us. We both felt duped and considered that each member of the workgroup could have been hand-picked by the Judiciary Committee to be a buffer from our cause. The special interests of supporting litigation and the bias toward women in sole custody disputes seemed to be their motivation. It felt obvious that it was not about the best interests and welfare of our children. I hoped we were wrong.

The psychologist and I needed to bypass the workgroup and reach the end-users of law: the judges. They were the referees in the cage fight of custody, not the promoters (the attorneys). We wanted to disprove the workgroup's claim that judges didn't want the choice to rule joint custody in contested cases. The psychologist mentioned that he knew a judge from our county that he planned to contact. His objective was to create a survey for the judge to distribute to their judicial peers. A few weeks later, the psychologist sent me a copy of the survey he had given to the judge:

> In an effort to write and submit a bill to the Oregon legislature that would allow judges to award joint legal custody in contested custody cases, we are attempting to collect data on whether judges would want to have the added option. Committee members have told us that judges no longer are receptive to considering the additional option and that they are not interested in that added ability. We have opted to approach the bench in Lane County to ascertain the relative truth of the assertion.
>
> Please answer the question by checking the appropriate box:
>
> ☐ As a Lane County Circuit Court Judge I would like to have the legal ability to award joint legal custody in contested cases.

☐ As a Lane County Circuit Court Judge I do not wish to have the legal ability to award joint legal custody in contested cases.

In advance, thank you for your time and consideration of this very important matter.

When the psychologist received the tally of the survey results from the judge, all of the judges that participated were in favor of having the ability to award joint legal custody in contested cases.

CHAPTER EIGHTEEN
# The Turn

In the fourth workgroup meeting, the psychologist held his independent and rogue survey results close to his chest. He and I were already walking on eggshells with the workgroup regarding the presumption of joint custody, and I figured that was his reason to stay silent. However, the psychologist had a much bigger surprise for the workgroup that was far more substantial than the private survey of circuit court judges. The agenda for this workgroup session was to read the family-law statutes of New Mexico, Texas, and Florida and to discuss anything we may find that would improve our state family law. It seemed to me that we should have been comparing the statutes from our neighboring states of California and Washington, which were also liberal, like Oregon.

Each of the three state's statutes were printed by the workgroup coordinator and stacked in piles on the conference room table. Our task was to read all the statutes and form our discussion points to share with the workgroup. As we all grabbed for the printouts, the psychologist recommended that we add to our sample group the reformed family law of Illinois, which had just implemented an unprecedented solution to legal custody. The state had scrubbed the inflammatory word *custody* from their statutes, and replaced it with *decision-making responsibilities.*

After the psychologist educated the workgroup about the progressive Illinois statutes (enacted January 1, 2016), it was difficult for the workgroup to focus on the three other state statutes in front of us. In fact, I can't recall anything about those statutes. I was only interested in the unprecedented solution of replacing custody all together, and I got tunnel vision. It was better than anything I had considered; it was a rational solution, and the chairman, Senate, and House had not "been there, done that!" Following the workgroup meeting, the psychologist and I reconvened outside the state capitol building again. I expressed my gratitude for his research and discovery of the Illinois statutes. He had given the workgroup and the state of Oregon a prospective way to give primary consideration to the best interests and welfare of our children.

The fifth workgroup meeting occurred a month later, and the coordinator had printed off copies of the Illinois Statutes. Under Allocations of Responsibilities, the 750 Illinois Compiled Statutes (ILCS) 5/602.5(d) states, "The court shall allocate decision-making responsibilities according to the child's best interests. Nothing in this Act requires that each parent be allocated decision-making responsibilities." This means that the court still has the power to allocate all the major decision-making responsibilities to one parent; the same result as sole custody. It is followed by 750 ILCS 5/602.5(b) which explains, "...the court shall allocate to one or both of the parents the significant decision-making responsibility for each significant issue affecting the child." The significant issues in Illinois are similar to the major decisions of custody in the state of Oregon. They are education, health, religion, and extracurricular activities.

Essentially, 750 ILCS 5/602.5(b) offers a way for the court to custom-tailor parenting arrangements on a case-by-case basis in the best interests of the child. It allows the court to allocate each of the significant issues to one or both parents. This is a rational alternative to the zero-sum game of sole custody that continues to damage families. The next step was to get the workgroup, Judiciary Committee, Senate, and members of the House to recognize the evident benefits of the Illinois reformed family-law statutes.

This workgroup meeting was different than other meetings. It was filled with collaboration, instead of division. Moreover, the workgroup member from the Oregon State Bar agreed to distribute a family-law survey to the organization's centers of influence around the state:

> Oregon State Bar
>
> Request to Comment or Take an Official Position on an Issue

Part 1

What is the issue under consideration? If there is pending legislation, what is the bill number, and what does the bill do?

Oregon family law recognizes the custodial parent as the person with primary decision-making authority over a minor child. Parenting time is the allocation of time one parent spends with the child. Separated parents may feel pressure or anxiety to assert themselves as the custodial parent in order to "win" over the other party. In practice, what many of these parents desire is more time with their children and some level of decision-making participation in the child's upbringing. Some states have already recognized that the term "custody" in itself creates an antagonistic situation in which parents vie for recognition as the custodial parent, regardless of the actual authority and parenting time that may come with it.

Recently, the state of Illinois revised its entire family-law code to remove the term *custody*. Instead, courts allocate *decision-making* authority on major issues to one or the other parent. For example, mother may be allocated decision-making authority on healthcare and extracurricular activities while father is allocated decision making on schooling and spiritual upbringing. Each tenet is either allocated by agreement of the parties or by the court if the parties fail to agree, using a "best interests of the child" standard. If both parents agree, the parents may share the decision-making authority for a particular tenet.

Additionally, Illinois removes the terms *custodial parent* and noncustodial parent and scrubs references to "visitation." Instead, each parent is allocated "parenting time" with no reference to a custodial parent or noncustodial parent. It may be that a court orders one parent to hold all decision-making authority and hold significantly more parenting time than another. But the parent is still not considered to have "sole custody" of the child.

The work group has examined this issue and would like further input from the Family Law Section of the Oregon State Bar on these two issues:

Should the terms *custody* and *visitation* be removed from the Oregon Revised Statutes and replaced with neutral terms, and if so, what terms should be used?

Should the major decision-making areas be divided amongst the parents, either by agreement or by the court, using the "best interests of the child" standard?

What position does your group wish to take? (For example: support, support with changes, express concerns, provide technical comments or feedback, etc.)

The workgroup supports the proposal to remove *custody* from the Oregon Revised Statutes and to clearly allow division of the tenets of parental decision making.

What are the biggest reasons your group is taking this position?

The group has had extensive discussions on the harm associated with creating a noncollaborative, zero-sum approach to family-law issues. The group supports this proposal because it will remove some of the competitive language embedded in the ORS and allow for greater flexibility in crafting parenting plans that reflect a reality that is in the best interests of the child.

What groups or constituencies would be most impacted or interested in this issue—who would support it and who would oppose it? Has your group had contact with the supporters of this proposal or issue?

This proposal would have wide-ranging impact on families, courts, family-law practitioners, legal services attorneys, and associated professionals who deal with family matters. This proposal is still in its infancy, and this request for review is the first outreach for feedback from a larger group of legal practitioners.

The last positive development of the fifth workgroup meeting was that the attorney from Salem mentioned that the annual Oregon State Bar family-law conference in Sisters, Oregon, was coming up. The guest speaker during the luncheon on the last day of the conference was going to be a highly regarded member of the Family Law Section of the Illinois State Bar Association (ISBA). She had played a major role in the reform of the Illinois family-law statutes, and I was determined to meet her. I wanted to hear her presentation that addressed the flaws of legal custody and learn from her.

At the end of the workgroup meeting, I asked the coordinator when we would meet again. She said that we would meet after the state bar collected the completed surveys from their centers of influence. The meeting was adjourned, and the psychologist and I met outside again to discuss the turn of events. We were excited by the new developments and cautiously optimistic about the new direction of the workgroup. We also discussed the irony that he had uncovered the reformed Illinois family-law statutes and not one of the members of the workgroup who had been hand-picked by the Judiciary Committee.

Since the attorney from Salem had conveyed to the workgroup the news of the guest speaker from Illinois, I emailed him to ask if I could attend the event. He committed to inquiring with organizers of the conference on my behalf and letting me know the result. As the conference date drew closer, I started pressing the attorney for an answer. I felt bad about my persistence, but he was my only point of contact, and I did not want to miss the opportunity to hear, and possibly meet, the presenter.

About a week before the conference, the attorney

from Salem emailed me an extended invitation from the event organizer. Since I covered the Central Oregon market in my occupation, I planned client meetings in that region for the day of the presentation. The evening before the conference, I received a call from the psychologist, who rarely called me unless it was important. He said that he was not able to attend the conference due to a conflict in his work schedule, but he had just finished a telephone conversation with the guest speaker. She understood our concerns on legal custody and felt strongly that custody was an inflammatory term that was dangerous and that it needed to be abolished.

The day of the conference, I started my drive to Sisters early in the morning. I took a road that followed along the McKenzie River and over the Cascade Mountain Range. I had my two dogs with me, and we made our traditional stop near the summit to quickly hike down to a misty waterfall. I was wearing my navy-blue power suit but I didn't care. The life inspiration of the natural setting was worth cleaning my shoes afterward, and it prepared my mindset for my mission at the conference: to learn from the guest speaker and apply that knowledge to my cause in the state of Oregon.

I continued my drive and arrived at the conference venue thirty minutes early. As I walked into the lobby, I saw two women sitting behind an elongated sign-in table. One of them stood up and asked me, "Are you Joseph?" She was the conference organizer who had invited me to the event. I said I was and continued toward her table. We introduced ourselves, and I shook the woman's hand from across the table. She handed me my name tag and introduced me to the woman on her right, who was still seated. She was the guest speaker from Illinois, waiting for her presentation to start.

The guest speaker stood up, and we shook hands. She asked if I would like to chat before the luncheon started. We walked along our sides of the table and met at the end where we could stand together and talk. The guest speaker explained her theory that everyone had a dark side and custody disputes were a major trigger of that side of ourselves. She told me to think of Anakin Skywalker becoming Darth Vader. This is what custody disputes could do to parents on the losing side, she suggested. She explained that it was also dangerous for the parents on the winning side because the losing parent could convert to a ticking time bomb. Legal custody disputes were a strong contributing factor to abusive, and sometimes fatal, scenarios. They were not the cure for domestic violence; they triggered it!

The luncheon where the guest speaker was presenting was in the dining lodge across the courtyard from the main lodge, where we were talking. As time got closer to lunch, we worked our way over to the venue, staying engaged in conversation. I discussed the resistance of the workgroup, which I believed stemmed from the Judiciary Committee. She understood my uphill battle. When we arrived at the dining lodge, there was a round table near the presentation podium that was reserved for an Oregon State Supreme Court justice, the Oregon State Bar workgroup member, the guest speaker from Illinois, and the event organizer. There was a vacant chair at the table, and the guest speaker asked the event organizer if I could sit there with her. I was offered a seat at their table by the organizer and gladly accepted the offer. It was a privilege to sit with such an esteemed group of influential public figures.

As I got comfortable in my seat, the guest speaker and I were still engaged in conversation. The state bar workgroup member arrived at the table, and I introduced her to the guest speaker. After the introduction, the workgroup member asked the speaker if it was difficult to scrub the language of custody from the old statutes. I leaned over to the speaker and whispered to her, "The resistance!" As the audience found their seats, salad was served. The guest speaker couldn't eat because she was nervous about her speech. Her condition reminded me that we were all human, from the Supreme Court justice to the dishwasher in the kitchen. As I started eating my salad, I recognized a conference participant who was walking toward me. It was the problematic husband of the attorney who represented Noni. As he passed my table, he focused on my name tag. He read my name, confirming my identity, and chuckled. I thought to myself, "In a primitive world, this guy would not survive. But in modern society, this guy could afford to have a Napoleon complex and thrive."

Before the main course was served, the event organizer stood up and walked over to the podium. She tested the mic and then gave an extensive introduction to the guest speaker from Illinois, which covered her background and success in transforming Illinois state family law. As the event organizer was giving the introduction, I asked the guest speaker if I could record her presentation. She welcomed the idea. As she walked up to the podium, I motioned a waitress over to my table. I got out my cell phone, engaged my audio memo application, and quietly asked her to place my phone near the podium.

The speaker started by saying that she was around when the series *Mad Men* was real.

"When it was *Mad Men*, there were words that were used to marginalize groups of people," she explained. "Since then, these groups of people have found their voice, and these words are no longer accepted in society, like the n-word and the q-word. The word that was used to marginalize divorced and never-married people and their children was the c-word. It was custody."

She paused to take a drink of water and then continued her speech.

"These types of words that have historically been used to marginalize people have an automatic effect. The automatic effect is that it takes a person from the prefrontal cortex part of their brain, where they can see nuance in possibility, into the reptilian part of the limbic system where all they can do is fight to survive. The power of the c-word is massive!"

The speaker discussed the etymology of the word *custody*, that it comes from the sixteenth-century English prison system.

"And we have remnants of it now," she explained. "Someone is taken into custody and they get periodic visitations. This word evokes a response that has been part of the culture for hundreds of years. The reaction is automatic. The body will sense it the same way it would sense being in close proximity to a predator type animal. The natural response is to guard one's territory. All of a sudden, we go from being a well-reasoned person like Dr. Jekyll, to Mr. Hyde."

She explained the solution from the state of Illinois.

"Instead of keeping *custody* as a code word or shorthand, they defined it. Then they used the definition instead of the label. It was defined as the responsibilities of making the major decisions for the child on healthcare, education, religion, and extracurricular activities. Now what we have is an allocation of responsibilities. It is what every other family has. They allocate responsibilities. Whether they are in a marriage or not, it shouldn't have to be in the bode of law. It's allocating responsibilities. Who is better able to assist in major decisions?" The speaker had attempted to reach the audience of family-law attorneys, who depended on litigation for financial success.

She added, "Most people don't disagree on major decisions."

I understood that she meant that most parents believe in western medicine, can find common ground on a belief system, desire a good education, and want their child to be involved in extracurricular activities.

"So, what is someone saying when they say they want

custody? Do they feel like they really need to be the one responsible in making all of the defined major decisions for their child because they are best suited to do so? Or, are they expressing their fear of loss, since they are no longer with the other parent? They trusted their judgement before, and they were wrong. Now they are having a panic attack not to trust their judgement again. They need to protect themselves. The other parent is going to get the keys to the kingdom, and they are going to be locked out and will freeze to death." This was the example she gave about why separations unravel into custody disputes. It wasn't really about the child's best interests. It was about fear!

"It hits the core of what people are all about. Attorneys are supposed to help parents through this transition," she professed. "Currently, custody is entitlement- and shame-based, with everything on the line."

The state of Illinois had successfully found what didn't work. Now the courts could help parents through the already difficult situation instead of throwing gasoline on the fire by staging a zero-sum game.

"Attorney's should be like midwives or sherpas in Tibet," the speaker included. "We are trying to get people from here to the next chapter with some degree of elegance, with some degree of belief that the future is not going to stink as much as the present does."

"The idea of judgement or being erased, only because a parent is insufficiently perfect or not an emotional ten, is absurd. The state of Illinois has changed the focus from shame and judgement to what works. It helps keep the balance in the family and the continued involvement of both parents in the child's life, if a tie breaker is needed."

Next, she compared legal-custody disputes to having a gigantic pot of soup on the stove—at high boil.

"If the soup falls onto the floor someone can get seriously scalded or may even die. The job of judges and attorneys is to have the tools to help drop the temperature and eliminate serious and sometimes fatal injury. It goes from a situation that feels like life and death to merely transitioning to a new phase in life. This can't be done with the current tools of the courts in the state of Oregon. The current tools promote volatile legal custody disputes where the end-user is terrified and living in survival mode. End-users feel like they are fighting for their lives, their futures, and their legacies."

The insightful and persuasive speaker concluded her poignant speech by repeating that the c-word is just like the n-word and just like the q-word.

"It has been a long time that this word needed to go away! People leaving relationships that involve children should not be punished, stigmatized, and ashamed. Nobody here is on such a high horse. Nobody here should be busy throwing stones," she exclaimed.

After the powerful speech, I gave the speaker a congratulatory hug and thanked her for setting the precedent of abolishing the c-word, a word that has hurt so many children, parents, and families.

CHAPTER NINETEEN
# A Voice

It has been almost five years since I started lobbying at the state level to help children, parents, and families. During this time, I have continued to witness my son's struggles in his current living arrangement. It is a helpless feeling for me, but I have learned to make the best of the time we have together and to recognize that his time with his mother (my non-parenting time) is out of my control. I had already tried to speak for him in court, but it was to no avail. My mindset has helped me cope with the unfortunate situation, but the guilt I feel for not helping my own son find resolution is eating away at me. Especially since he has asked me on many occasions, "Why can't I talk to a judge?" and, as explained in the statute that the attorney from Salem shared with me, I've known of a way that he can.

My desire to help my son has been channeled into lobbying, but the pending bill will not help my son in his current situation. Custody has already been decided, and Noni will never agree to lose time with him. I assume her reasons have to do with her false feelings of abandonment and her need for control. Her reasons are certainly not about my son's best interests and welfare; she is fully aware of their constant struggles together. If someone was to ask her why she will not agree to allow him more time where he is thriving, she would probably blame their difficulties on me. There would be no admission from her of being culpable for their difficulties together.

In the state of Oregon, there is no legal age where a minor can have a legal voice about their best interests and welfare. In the state of California, the legal age when a child has a voice with the court is fourteen years old. However, California just introduced the Giving Children a Voice Act which will allow children the same right to address the court at age ten. It is progress, but it isn't in my state. The state of Oregon takes pride in the progressive and liberal mindset of its people, but it needs to support its children better. There are major gaps in current state law versus the best interests and welfare of our children.

While I have been lobbying, I have been a parent and a full-time employee with a demanding job. An opportunity presented itself again for me to visit the foreign exchange family I lived with in Brazil in high school. I found a window of time where I would not miss any time with my son. The trip was amazing as always! My foreign exchange family was wonderful, the food was great, and the weather was hot. I also had some great adventures that helped me disconnect from the stress of work and the uphill battle of lobbying for my cause. Two of the memorable adventures were visiting a famous contemporary art museum in the forest, and hiking through amazing caverns in a national park that had not yet been opened to the public. Something else that happened on this trip was that I was unable to communicate with my son. It wasn't unusual that my calls to him were not answered, but it really affected me this time. Maybe it was due to the geographical challenge I had and that I didn't have an alternate way to check in on him and tell him I loved and missed him. Since we were not able to speak on my trip, I wrote a poem and handed it to him when I returned home. It sounds cliché, but it was cathartic for me and it let him know that I was thinking about him:

> *Hello Son. How are you today?*
> *I sure miss your smile and playing soccer all the day.*
> *One day you will have a say to talk to who you want any time of day.*
> *Until then, from one to ten,*
> *When you are at the zoo, how are the zebras looking after you?*
> *I know that one day you will go a long way.*
> *Just remember to take it day by day.*
> *And in the end, you will have a friend any time of day*
> *To do what we want and play the way we play.*
> *I'm always counting down the time when you'll be fine*
> *And won't have to hide under your bed with me on the line.*
> *You are the best! The best of the best! Better than the rest!*

*I love you so much! I miss you so much!
So please stay tough through the time that is rough!*

He read the poem aloud and proudly. It meant so much to him and even more to me! The metaphor of the zebras in the zoo was about Noni. We had previously created code language on the phone so I could merely ask him how he was doing without Noni getting offended while she listened closely to our dialog. The alphabet was our range, and the first letter of a word was our meter. However, Noni broke our code one day when I asked him how he was doing and he said, "I'm with the zebras at the zoo."

My trip to Brazil helped me gain clarity on what was important when I returned home. The bill needed to be written before the next legislative session, my son needed to be heard, and I needed to re-establish myself financially to plan for his future. Upon my return home, I resumed my campaign.

I had not communicated with the chairman of the Judiciary Committee since the judiciary hearing, and it seemed like an appropriate time to meet with him again to discuss the workgroup from my perspective. I contacted his office and his assistant scheduled a meeting for us to meet at a local boutique food pavilion. But after I arrived, the chairman never showed up. I contacted his assistant, who rescheduled a new date and a different venue. This time we would meet at the old coffee shop where we met before. Also, I invited the psychologist to join us this time.

The psychologist and I met inside the coffee shop, and the chairman arrived moments later. We sat down at the closest table and started our discussion. Our time was limited, so there was no time for drinks. Once we were seated, I placed a picture of my son down on the table to remind the chairman why we were there. It wasn't for the best interests and welfare of attorneys, politicians, or even judges. It was for the best interests of children!

In our meeting, we discussed the resistance of the workgroup and the recent intelligence the psychologist had uncovered regarding the reformed Illinois family-law statutes. I also mentioned the Oregon State Bar survey that was pending and the next workgroup meeting that was nowhere in sight. I was concerned that our time was expiring and that we could potentially miss our window to get the bill drafted for the legislative session, which was approaching quickly. Before we finished our meeting, the chairman gave us his word that the bill would be drafted before the next legislative session, and it would be discussed by the Senate and the House. He also mentioned that he would follow up with the workgroup coordinator, who was the point person for producing the bill, to make sure we were on track.

Following our meeting, I emailed the workgroup coordinator and summarized the chairman's commitment to the bill. I also suggested that maybe it was not necessary for the workgroup to meet again if we already established that the bill would be based on the Illinois statutes. The coordinator responded to my email and confirmed she had submitted a bill request on the Illinois language and that she was waiting for the draft to be completed. She said that once the draft was completed, the workgroup would reconvene to read and discuss the bill.

I had covered my bases with the chairman and the coordinator of the workgroup. If the bill was passed, it would help so many families, but it would not help my son. It was time to advocate for him again to have a legal voice of his own. He is almost five years older than when I went to court and spoke for him, and his maturity level is higher than most ten-year-old boys. He will turn eleven next month.

I thought of the Oregon statute that the attorney from Salem shared with me. It would allow my son the opportunity to have a legal voice. If I didn't tell him about the statute, I was enabling his constant suffering in his other home. It wasn't about sour grapes between Noni and I, it was about his strained relationship with his mother. He was vocal with his last therapist (the psychologist), and I wanted to meet with his new therapist to get his opinion of my son's current situation.

The new therapist was a young gentleman, and my son really liked him. They had played sports and card games, which helped their rapport. When I met the therapist for the first time in person, he said two things that were parallel with the last therapist's opinions: my son desperately wanted more time in my care, and my son didn't need the constant therapy. It seemed that the therapy was more for Noni's sake, which was also consistent with the past.

I told the therapist that I was considering explaining to my son the statute that would allow him to have a legal voice. The therapist responded by saying that he had been working diligently with Noni to allow him to have more overnights with me. I was certain she was incapable of allowing my son more time in my care because she saw it as losing control. If she had given the therapist any hope, it was false hope. The therapist understood why I had my beliefs but said that he would remain hopeful of her acceptance. He was my son's advocate, and he knew how badly my son wanted to spend more time in my care. He also knew I was a good father from what my son had shared with him.

Notifying my son of the statute was a big decision. I faced a dilemma: should I allow him to continue suffering in his current environment or should I expose him to litigation against his own mother? Besides, within the courtroom, Noni would distort his desire to spend more time in my care into my culpability for their struggles. The difference this time would be that my son could speak firsthand to the court. I needed to let my decision marinate a little longer.

A few days later, I was at a business meeting downtown and ran into a work acquaintance who was a financial advisor. Seeing him reminded me that I needed to re-evaluate my retirement plan and open a new college fund for my son. So, we scheduled a meeting to discuss my financial goals. Before our meeting started, we discussed our world travels. He was originally from Spain, and we both enjoyed visiting new places. Then we moved on and discussed my retirement plan and creating a new college fund for my son, which then led us to our next topic of conversation—our children. He and his wife had two young children, and I shared with him that I was a single parent. I also mentioned that I used to have a college fund for my son, but I had to liquidate it to pay off attorneys after unsuccessfully trying to secure more time with him.

After I exposed my personal baggage to the financial advisor, he became passionate about my son's unfortunate situation. He insisted that I contact a member of his running club, who was an old-timer family-law attorney who, in his prime, could run a sub-four-minute mile. He also mentioned that the attorney worked in his profession for the right reasons—to help children. At first, I told him I wasn't interested in meeting any more attorneys and that I had learned my lesson from the last go around. But then I thought about it more and realized I should meet with him to discuss my dilemma about my son getting his own attorney to represent him. I jotted down the attorney's contact information, and we got back to discussing my finances. When I left the meeting, it felt like there had been another purpose to it: to help me gain clarity on how to successfully advocate for my son in the court of law. It was the only way his voice would be heard and accepted.

    I contacted the attorney's office right after our meeting and scheduled an appointment with his assistant. I was anxious to speak with him regarding the statute that could give my son a legal voice. When I met with the attorney, he was unaware that the statute existed. He thumbed through the state family-law statutes and found the statute I spoke of. He was embarrassed that he didn't know of the statute, but he didn't need to be. I was appreciative of any legal advice he could give me to help my son.

After discussing the statute, the attorney recommended that he write Noni's attorney a letter, requesting that her client consider an adjustment in the parenting schedule to accommodate our son's wishes to spend more time in my care. He added that my son had been forcefully expressing his feelings to both parents, and to others, and he had indicated a strong desire to spend more time with me. The attorney also confirmed in the letter that I was willing to accommodate my son's request, and that I wasn't forcing him into expressing his preference.

Ample time had passed for the other attorney to respond to the letter, but she hadn't. I knew that would be the outcome, so I was prepared for the letdown. My new attorney and I met again, and he expressed a desire to meet my son firsthand to gauge his maturity level. At the next meeting, I brought my son in with me and introduced him to the attorney. From there, I left the room to give them privacy. An hour later the attorney invited me back into his office. He spoke in front of my son and said that my son was capable of speaking for himself in a courtroom. He also acknowledged that my son had communicated what he desperately desired: to spend more time in my care. We discussed the statute with my son, and he was motivated to write a letter asking the court to appoint him an attorney. At the end of our meeting, my attorney said that he would start the paperwork to file a motion with the court to modify parenting time.

It was a two-step process. First came the motion to modify parenting time and second came the letter from my son to the presiding judge. My attorney created a case number with the court, and my son wrote his letter. It explained that he wanted more time in my care, that his mother wasn't allowing it to happen, and that he struggled in his mother's care. He needed an attorney to help him have a voice. The letter now sits in a drawer in my office because I fear how Noni will handle the new development of him having his own legal voice. Until now, he has been kept quiet in a court of law. Noni's attorney scheduled our hearing date six months out, just as she had done the last time I petitioned for more parenting time. My son's letter will be sent when the trial date gets closer. I want to minimize the time between the trial date and when Noni finds out about his request.

My son will be eleven years old by the set trial date; he has suffered enough! My concern of him going to court is present, but letting him continue to suffer is culpable. He has wanted a legal voice for so long, and he will finally get his opportunity to have one.

CHAPTER TWENTY
# A Better Way

My campaign for children's rights, parental equality, and family balance has progressed from thought into action. I spoke my voice and my voice was heard. My belief is that children should not be placed between two parents in a dispute and be awarded to the winner. Parents should not be legally disenfranchised from their children simply due to a loaded disagreement. And families should not lose their integrity and balance due to a zero-sum game.

At the beginning of my campaign, I needed to find an alternative solution to custody disputes that the state had not already considered. My solution was to empower the court with the ability to rule joint custody in contested cases. The court could assign each of the major decision-making responsibilities to the most appropriate parent, instead of an all-or-nothing scenario. It was a rational solution that would ensure parental involvement and preserve family balance for the child, without requiring the parents to rely on making decisions together.

However, the state of Illinois implemented a better solution than mine. They removed the entitlement- and shame-based c-word altogether and replaced it with the term *decision-making responsibilities*. What's more, they identified those responsibilities, and they can now be allocated to either one, or both parents. By allocating each of the responsibilities, the court can give primary consideration to the best interests and welfare of the child and avoid the zero-sum game of legal custody disputes.

Domestic violence is a serious concern, and victims must be protected. The Illinois statutes allow the court to protect victims (spouses and children) by allocating all the responsibilities to the nonabusive parent, just as in sole custody. However, the Illinois statutes also allow the court to custom-tailor parenting arrangements for parents who simply don't get along. This way, parents cannot be legally disenfranchised from their children because the other parent has decided to hijack parenthood.

Attorneys should be advocates and consultants for families and assist in creating smooth transitions from one household into two loving homes. The zealous representation of fight-or-flight parents—putting everything on the line—is irrational. The Illinois statutes allow attorneys the option to negotiate and compromise, instead of joint, all, or nothing. These options are too rigid and do not allow for both parents to have their own major decision-making responsibilities. There is a reason parents separate, and it is presumptuous of the court to insist that either they work together, or one parent loses their parental rights.

Legal custody initiates the entitlement of absolute control and the fear of being erased. It is a catalyst for the zero-sum game. In fact, custody disputes could be considered a non-zero-sum game. The winner maintains their custodial rights, while the loser is stripped of theirs. The loser loses much more than the winner wins.

The shame-filled label of noncustodial parent has discriminated against me and my son for most of his life. The hypocrisy of family law is the reason for this. Oregon Revised Statute 107.137(1) claims, "The court shall give primary consideration to the best interests and welfare of a child," but the claim is impossible to implement due to ORS 107.169(3), which states, "The court shall not order joint custody, unless both parents agree to the terms and conditions of the order." In my case, Noni insisted on sole custody, and I lost the fight I didn't want. Since then, I have aspired to advocate for children's rights, parental equality, and family balance to give future transitioning families a better roadmap than the one my family had.

The legislative session started on February 1, 2017 in Oregon, and the bill to abolish the c-word will be discussed by the Oregon Senate and House of Representatives. This legislative session may last up to 160 days, and I must raise awareness now. This is not an issue that should fly under the radar and only be discussed by the Senate and the House. This is a civil-rights issue that should be discussed by everyone who has been marginalized by family law that is broken.

Throughout my campaign, I have made a few allies, but in large part I have been on my own. Now I am at the crossroads, as the rest of my story is ahead of me. I can either wait for the conclusion to unfold, or I can attempt to affect the conclusion by raising awareness through my story now. My story isn't unique or special. In fact, stories like mine are far too common, and they need to have a just and fair ending. If you, or someone you know, has been negatively affected by legal custody, please contact your local congressperson and make your voice heard. Even if my story is read after this legislative session, or you are from another state or different country, it is never too late to have a voice for your cause.

My goal for the future is to write a new story. A story about how the c-word was recognized for the harm that it causes and how it is no longer tolerated. Families will no longer be exposed to the potential weapon of custody, which can rip them apart. Instead, they can rely on the court to allocate each of the major decision-making responsibilities to the most appropriate parent. I also hope to discuss the implementation of a cooling period and parenting coordinators for families who need them. Families deserve the proper tools to assist them through transitioning from one home into two loving households with integrity and balance. Lastly, I hope to write about my son attaining what he deserves by having the right to use his own voice to effect positive change in his life.

Made in the USA
San Bernardino, CA
18 March 2017